KANT

KANT

Stephan Körner

NEW HAVEN AND LONDON
YALE UNIVERSITY PRESS

First published in 1955 in the United Kingdom in a paperback edition
by Penguin Books Limited. Published in 1982 in the United States
of America by Yale University Press.

Printed in the United States of America.

Library of Congress Cataloging in Publication Data

Körner, Stephan, 1913-
  Kant.
  Bibliography: p.
  Includes index.
  1. Kant, Immanuel, 1724-1804.   I. Title.
B2798.K6   1982   193   81-16120
ISBN 0-300-02792-3 (pbk.)   AACR2

10 9 8 7 6 5 4 3 2 1

It is much easier to point out the faults and
errors in the work of a great mind than to
give a distinct and full exposition
of its value.

SCHOPENHAUER
Criticism of the Kantian Philosophy

CONTENTS

NOTE

This book was originally published in a Pelican series
devoted to the history and problems of philosophy and
has been continuously in print since 1955. The present edition is unchanged, except for some updating of
the bibliographical appendices.

THE translations of passages of Kant are my own, though I have tried to keep the available standard English translations in mind. References throughout are to the *Akademie* edition of Kant's works, the following being the abbreviations employed:

Pu. R. *Critique of Pure Reason* (text of the 2nd edition)
Pr. R. *Critique of Practical Reason*
Ju. *Critique of Judgement*
Prol. *Prolegomena to every Future Metaphysic*
Gr. *Groundwork of the Metaphysic of Morals*
Rel. *Religion within the Limits of Pure Reason*

Others of Kant's works are referred to by the number of the volume in the *Akademie* edition. The following abbreviations are also used:

B *Critique of Pure Reason*, 2nd edition, Königsberg, 1787
Ab Abbott's translation of the *Critique of Practical Reason* and other ethical works.

Some English translations which are at present easily available are listed in Appendix B.

In fulfilment of the task assigned to me to produce a short book on Kant, I have tried to offer what is strictly an introduction; and one which, on the other hand, seeks to confine itself to the *critical* philosophy, as found – to the best of my belief – in Kant's mature work beginning with the *Critique of Pure Reason*.

Naturally I have not aimed at completeness; and in deciding what to touch upon and what to omit, I have consistently tried to give priority to those of Kant's problems to which his approach has still a present-day interest, as distinct from those whose interest, by now, is probably chiefly historical. I shall have achieved a great part of my purpose if I have succeeded in whetting any philosophical reader's appetite for Kant's own words, or that of any reader at all for philosophy in general.

Preface

Dr A. C. Ewing, Professor J. W. Scott, and the Editor of the series have read the book in typescript and have made many helpful suggestions and criticisms; and I have profited much from conversations with Professor G. C. Field on Kant's moral theory. Professor Scott has been good enough also to undertake the laborious and thankless task of improving the English of an earlier version and has thereby rendered me, and indeed my readers, an invaluable service. I should also like to thank my friend Mr Basil Cottle for sacrificing his time to helping me read the proofs. It gives me great pleasure to thank these philosophers and scholars publicly for their kindness and help. The responsibility for the book rests, of course, entirely with myself.

STEPHAN KÖRNER

1954

CHAPTER ONE

THE PLAN OF THE CRITICAL PHILOSOPHY

1. The Metaphysical Impulse

THE name metaphysics is apt to suggest something difficult, unusual, and remote. Yet it has its familiar side. Most of us have times at which, in reflection, we seem to be confronted not with any particular isolated problem or any particular aspect of our experience but with experience, or life, or existence, *as a whole.* These might be called our metaphysical moments. It is not easy to give a detailed description of them and for our purpose it is not necessary. Indirectly and roughly, however, it is possible to identify them by saying that if they did not occur there would be no point in religion and little in many works of art and philosophy.

Those who, at least in our culture, reflect upon their metaphysical moods tend to be driven to what are, or seem to be, questions of profound importance about the meaning of life: about death and immortality, about moral freedom and natural necessity, about the existence of God. Compared with these – real or apparent – metaphysical questions, even the most complex and far-reaching problems of natural science and mathematics may seem insignificant and even trivial.

I have been careful to speak of real or apparent metaphysical questions, not simply of metaphysical questions, and have to give reasons for my caution. In doing so I shall be formulating a philosophical problem which, as it happens, was the central problem of Kant, and still is a major preoccupation of contemporary philosophy. For this purpose I shall, first of all, quite roughly, exhibit some differences between questions of mathematics and natural science on the one hand and those of metaphysics on the other.

There are many mathematical questions to which the answers are not known. Yet we, or the mathematical experts among us, do know, when an answer is proposed, how to set about deciding whether it is acceptable. To be so it must be proved. It must be shown to be derivable in accordance with certain well-defined methods of mathematical procedure. Without these methods there could be no science of mathematics. In a similar manner there are fairly well-defined methods of natural science in accordance with which the acceptability of a scientific hypothesis is decided by us or by the experts among us.

Needless to say, the methods by which mathematical theorems are proved and those by which the acceptability of a scientific hypothesis is established differ greatly. Nor are the methods always so sharply defined as to exclude the possibility of controversy about them between experts. Yet it is a remarkable fact that experts in mathematics and the natural sciences do frequently agree about the acceptability or otherwise of proposed answers to questions arising in their several fields.

We may indeed say that a body of statements (or an inquiry resulting in statements) is not a science unless it possesses a method by which the acceptability of its statements is tested. This is not of course sufficient to make a system of statements, or an inquiry, into a science: for then if the practitioners of graphology and astrology only decided to adopt certain methods of deriving, say, analyses of character from handwriting and prophecies from the mutual positions of the stars, they would be scientists. There must plainly be some further characteristics by which the sciences are distinguished from pseudo-sciences and non-sciences in general.

However, it must already, even without looking for such further marks of a science, appear sufficiently doubtful whether an inquiry concerning immortality, freedom, God and other such metaphysical issues can be in any sense a science: for while metaphysicians dispute, as scientists also do, as to whether this or that account gives the right answer to a certain problem, the metaphysicians dispute without even any agree-

ment among them as to how they would recognize the right
answer if they met it.

Let us then, at least for the moment, assume that metaphysics
is not a science. This does not mean that metaphysics could
never become one. For all we know it may still be in its in-
fancy because its proper methods may not yet have been separated from alien or spurious principles. After all, the science of
mathematics itself had, for very long, its proper principles
almost inextricably mixed with empirical rules of thumb; and
the separation of natural science from magic was a comparatively late achievement of mankind.

Yet, on the other hand, the scientific prospects of metaphysics seem pretty precarious. It seems somehow incapable
of ever becoming a science. What it calls its questions may
lack all theoretical significance. While appearing to be questions, they may be merely expressions of moods as some sighs
are, and some poems and symphonies. If this turned out to be
all they were then it would still be a most important anthropo-
logical fact that we are at times overcome by metaphysical
moods in which we appear to be questioning – when in truth
we are not really asking anything.

In Kant's time and, in spite of Kant's life-work, in our own
time, too, many acute and powerful thinkers believe, teach,
and indeed preach that metaphysics is a body of meaningless
sentences and an inquiry which can only lead us to the utter-
ance of such sentences. Hume says in an often quoted passage:
'If we take in our hand any volume; of divinity or school metaphysics, for instance, let us ask; *Does it contain any abstract reasoning concerning quantity or number?* No. *Does it contain any experimental reasoning concerning matter of fact and existence?* No.
Commit it then to the flames: for it can contain nothing but
sophistry and confusion.'[1] Essentially the same view is, in less
exciting prose, expressed by the contemporary logician R.
Carnap: 'The suppositious sentences of metaphysics, of the
philosophy of values, of ethics . . . are pseudo-sentences, they

1. *An Enquiry Concerning Human Understanding*, Selby-Bigge,
p. 165.

have no logical content, but are only expressions of feeling which in their turn stimulate feelings and volitional tendencies on the part of the hearer.'[1]

Kant in his so-called pre-critical period had accepted Hume's argument and had convinced himself that metaphysics – in particular all speculation about the three great metaphysical questions of God, Freedom, and Immortality – was waste of time. This conviction he expressed above all in a book whose title is a concise summary of its contents: *Dreams of a Ghost-Seer, elucidated by Dreams of Metaphysics* (1766). He never, even in later years, after the idea of the critical philosophy had taken hold of him, ceased to admire Hume's philosophical acumen. For his anti-metaphysical argument he remained avowedly grateful. It had taught him that whoever wishes to engage in a metaphysical inquiry must first be clear about the nature of the undertaking, especially the logical status of metaphysical propositions and the methods of establishing their acceptability. Before indulging in metaphysics we need a critique of reason to show how far or in what sense it is a possibility. We need, at least, to quote the title of another of his books, certain *Prolegomena to any Future Metaphysic which is to rank as a Science* (1783).

The effect of Hume's attack had been a clearing of the air and a sharpening of the analytical powers of Hume's philosophical followers and opponents. In our own time Carnap and the logical positivist movement to which he belongs have had a similar salutary effect. If Kant's answer to Hume, whether right or wrong, was relevant to the issues raised by Hume's scepticism, then it will be relevant to the very similar issues raised by modern logical positivists, however much more powerful their logical and analytical armoury may have become in the years since Kant's death. Thus, so far from leading to the graveyard of philosophical problems, an introduction to Kant's philosophy may hope to lead to questions which are still alive and important. It might even, with luck, serve as an introduction to philosophy.

1. *Logical Syntax of Language*, London, 1937, p. 279.

2. Kant's Classification of Judgements

The argument of Hume and the logical positivists against metaphysics rests on two statements, one of a logical distinction, the other of a definition. The distinction is the statement that metaphysical propositions are neither empirical nor analytic propositions. That is to say, they are neither propositions which are verifiable or falsifiable by experiment or observation, such as 'The top of Chimborazo is white' or 'Cooking salt is soluble in water'. Nor are they propositions whose denials are self-contradictory, such as 'A rainy day is a wet day' or 'If all men are mortal and Socrates is a man, then Socrates is mortal'. Now it seems clear enough that, e.g. 'God exists', 'Man is morally responsible' and other such statements are not empirical; and they are not analytic. On this point there is almost general agreement, and Kant certainly did not wish to dispute it.

The definition gives a meaning of the term 'meaningful proposition': it defines a meaningful proposition as one which is either empirical or analytic. If we agree with the distinction and if we accept the definition, then we must conclude that metaphysical propositions are meaningless.

The anti-metaphysical argument is easily learned and applied. In the thirties of the present century it gave much pleasure to undergraduates; and, among philosophers, whose views were more complex, less streamlined, and less adapted to concise formulation, it probably caused equally great annoyance. The game went like this. 'You say that man has an immortal soul. Before we go into that, I should like to consider a preliminary question, namely: what sort of statement is this you are making? It surely is not empirical. We cannot possibly make experiments or observations which would verify or falsify it. Again, it is certainly not analytic: for to assert that man has *not* an immortal soul, is not to commit the mistake of a contradiction in terms. So the proposition, or rather the alleged proposition, being neither empirical nor analytic, is meaningless. The question: is it false or is it true cannot arise. Next problem, please!'

It interests us to consider the second premiss of the anti-metaphysical argument a little more closely. If the person who defines a meaningful proposition as one which is empirical or analytic thereby merely wishes to propose a new usage for the term 'meaningful', we can hardly object to his proposal, although we need not adopt it. If, however, the definition is supposed to record an established use then it is mistaken. To show this briefly let us take an example or two of the sort of proposition which would generally be regarded as meaningful and which yet is neither empirical nor analytic. 'Pay your taxes!', 'Do as you would be done by' and any other normative proposition could serve as the required counter-example. A normative proposition is, of course, different from a statement of fact or logic; but it is not, therefore, meaningless in the sense in which, say, 'Virtue is triangular' might be so regarded.

Kant does not accept the Humean dichotomy of meaningful propositions, because he believes that as a matter of fact we are 'in possession of' propositions which fall into neither of Hume's two classes; they form a third class whose logical nature, function, and systematic connexion with each other and with other types of proposition is the main topic of his own philosophy. This Kantian classification of propositions has been the subject of many unfavourable comments, some critics going so far as to see in it the root of a mistake which vitiates the whole critical philosophy. To this classification we now turn, and before commenting upon it I shall try to expound it.

Kant's classification is, first of all, not of propositions, but of judgements, i.e. of propositions asserted by somebody. He is concerned not with the proposition that the cat is on the mat but with the judgement by some person to that effect. This is in many ways an advantage, since judgements are personal events, and the manner in which they exist is less problematic than the manner of existence of propositions.

Every judgement, says Kant, is either analytic or synthetic. 'In all judgements in which the relation of a subject to a pre-

dicate is thought ... this relation is possible in two different
ways. Either the predicate B belongs to the subject A, as
something which is (covertly) contained in this concept A; or
B lies outside the concept A, although it does indeed stand in
connexion with it. In the one case I call the judgement *analytic*,
and the other *synthetic*.'[1] For example, in the judgement that a
rainy day is a wet day the predicate 'wet day' is *contained* in the
subject 'rainy day', that is to say, the assertion that a rainy day
is not a wet day is a contradiction in terms. On the other hand
in the judgement that a rainy day is a cold day the predicate
'cold day' is not contained in the subject 'rainy day', that is to
say, the assertion that a rainy day is not cold is not a contradiction in terms. The former proposition is thus analytic, the
latter synthetic. Analytic propositions merely elucidate the
meaning of terms but are otherwise uninformative.

Further, a judgement is for Kant either *a priori* or *a posteriori*.
A judgement is *a priori* if it 'is independent of all experience
and even of all impressions of the senses'.[2] The independence
in question is logical. Two judgements are logically independent if neither of them entails either the other or the contradictory of it; and if the same is true also of their contradictories. For example, 'This flower is red' does not entail that
the sun is shining or that it is not shining. Hence 'This flower
is red' and 'The sun is shining' are logically independent; on the
other hand, 'This flower is red' and 'This flower is yellow' are
logically dependent. Each logically entails the negation of the
other. Now if a judgement is to be *a priori* it must be logically
independent of all judgements which describe experiences or
even impressions of sense. Examples are the judgement that
$2 + 2 = 4$, that an equiangular Euclidean triangle is necessarily
equilateral, that every father is necessarily male. It is of course
true that these judgements have a kind of dependence on experience. We form them as a result of certain experiences and in
the course of reacting to them. However, this dependence is not
what is meant by logical dependence. The above *a priori* judgements would be equally true in a world having no separate

1. *Pu. R.* 33, *B* 10.   2. *Pu. R.* 28, *B* 2.

countable objects, no shapes, and no differences of sex. They are logically independent of any such judgements as would describe that world, or any other experienced world.

Judgements which are not *a priori* are *a posteriori*, i.e. they depend logically on other judgements which describe experiences or impressions of sense. Not only judgements which describe a particular experience or sense-impression are *a posteriori*. Even general judgements may be logically dependent on such descriptions and therefore *a posteriori*. For example the judgement that *all* bodies, if deprived of support, fall downwards is *a posteriori* because it entails the description of particular observable experiences.

Kant's classification seems at first sight to permit the four possibilities: synthetic *a posteriori*, synthetic *a priori*, analytic *a priori*, analytic *a posteriori*. Of those the fourth possibility must be ruled out. There can be no analytic *a posteriori* judgements. An analytic proposition, being only about the meaning of terms, does not give us any other information. An *a posteriori* proposition, being dependent on experience, does. This leaves us with three classes of judgement which Kant holds to be not only possible but abundantly exemplified in our thinking.

All analytic judgements must be *a priori* since they merely elucidate the meaning of their terms and are thus logically independent of judgements describing sense-experience. If analytic judgements are necessarily *a priori*, then all that are *a posteriori* (non *a priori*) are necessarily synthetic (non-analytic). Both the Humeans and the logical positivists would agree with Kant that there are analytic *a priori* and synthetic *a posteriori* judgements.

We now turn to the last possibility, synthetic *a priori* judgements, i.e. judgements whose predicates are *not* contained in their subjects and which yet are logically independent of all judgements describing sense-experience. Kant holds that there are such; that almost the whole of mathematics consists of them and that they constitute the fundamental presuppositions of the natural sciences and of moral thought. It will be best to consider some examples of what Kant regarded as synthetic *a priori* judgements and to explain his reasons for so regarding them.

Consider first the arithmetical judgement that the addition of 5 to 7 yields 12. That this proposition is *a priori* would be readily agreed. Kant, however, regards it as at the same time synthetic since 'the concept of a sum of 7 and 5 contains nothing over and above the uniting of both these numbers into a single one'. It does in particular not imply any answer to the question as to 'which this number is which unites the two'.[1] In order to understand Kant's point we must, I think, realize that the addition of 5 to 7 is for him a process in time from whose description we cannot *deduce* its result, although we are on other grounds absolutely sure of it. In an analogous way in the world of sense-experience we cannot *deduce* from a person's having been shot through the heart that he will die although on other grounds we may be almost certain of it.

We turn next to the judgement 'Every change has a cause'. This is *a priori* since it does not entail any proposition which describes a sense-experience (or the negation of such a proposition). And it is synthetic since its negation, that there is uncaused change (e.g. a mere succession of different impressions), is not self-contradictory. Whether we could have a science of nature without judging that every change must have a cause is an altogether different question. To it Kant's answer is emphatically 'No'.

The last example is taken from a different field of thought again, namely the ethical judgement that what we ought to do is determined by the moral law (and not by our motives and desires which may run contrary to it). This judgement is synthetic: to deny it by stating that our duty is not determined by any absolute moral law but by natural causes may be true or false, but is not self-contradictory. It is also *a priori* since what ought to be does not entail any factual judgement to the effect that something is or is not the case at any moment of time.

To sum up: Kant replaces the positivist dichotomy of judgements into empirical and logically necessary by the trichotomy

1. *Pu. R.* 37, *B* 15.

of (1) analytic *a priori*, (2) synthetic *a posteriori*, (3) synthetic *a priori* judgements. In so far as metaphysical judgements are meaningful – such is the Kantian position – they must fall within this third class. The class, however, is one which contains other kinds of proposition also, e.g. 'Two and two are four'.

3. Kant's Conception of Synthetic *A Priori* Judgements

The critical philosophy is essentially an inquiry into the nature and function of synthetic *a priori* judgements. Its main task 'is contained in the question: How are synthetic *a priori* judgements possible?'[1] If there are no such judgements then Kant's central question formulates a pseudo-problem, and his answer is but another dream of another ghost-seer. If, short of this, these judgements are not as he conceives them, then the misconception must indicate a flaw in the fundamental structure of his thought.

The main objections to this Kantian distinction between synthetic and analytic judgements are first that Kant considers only subject-predicate judgements and secondly that his definition of an analytic judgement as one whose subject *contains* its predicate is metaphorical and therefore too vague. Although both objections are justified, I do not believe either is so serious as may seem at first sight. It is perfectly true that the subject of a judgement cannot contain its predicate in the same sense in which one box can contain another. But Kant's meaning is clear: the subject of a judgement *contains* its predicate if, and only if, the negation of the judgement is a contradiction in terms. To say metaphorically that in the judgement 'Green is a colour', 'colour' is contained in 'green' is merely to say that by denying of green that it is a colour we are contradicting ourselves.

In drawing the distinction between analytic and synthetic

1. *Pu. R.* 39, *B* 19.

judgements, though not in the remainder of his work, Kant certainly neglects judgements which are not of the subject-predicate form. He does not comment on the difference between, e.g. 'Socrates is a man' or 'The grass is green', which are, and, e.g. 'If the sun shines, then it is warm' or '*a* is greater than *b*' which are not of this form. Neither does he say why for his purposes the apparent difference does not matter. This strange omission on his part might be explained by his acceptance of almost the whole of traditional logic, which concerned itself mainly with subject-predicate propositions.

While it might be interesting to look for historical explanations, it is right to ask also whether Kant's definition of analytic judgements could not be applied to judgements not of subject-predicate form. This extension is easy and natural, and conforms, as I believe, to Kant's intentions. We have seen that a subject-predicate proposition, e.g. 'Every father is male', is analytic if, and only if, its subject *contains* its predicate or, speaking without metaphor, if, and only if, the denial of the proposition is a contradiction in terms. Now the denial of a proposition may be a contradiction in terms even if the proposition is not of subject-predicate form. For example the denial of 'If *a* is greater than *b* then *b* is smaller than *a*' is certainly a contradiction in terms. The proposition on the other hand does not tell us anything that is not 'contained' in its terms.

We thus arrive at the following reconstruction of the Kantian distinction between synthetic and analytic judgements, one which no longer restricts it to subject-predicate judgements or indeed to judgements of any particular form. A judgement is analytic if, and only if, its denial would be a contradiction in terms or, what amounts to the same, if it is *logically* necessary or, again in other words, if its negation is *logically* impossible. A judgement which is not analytic is synthetic. This reconstructed distinction of all propositions into analytic and synthetic is accepted by contemporary logicians almost generally although, needless to add, it is not wholly unproblematic or as unproblematic as I shall assume it to be.

I now turn to the radical criticism, the allegation that no judgement can possibly be both *a priori* and synthetic. This objection is based on a confusion by Kant's critics, and by some of his commentators, of at least two senses of the term 'necessary': a narrower sense in which only analytic propositions are necessary and a wider sense in which all *a priori* propositions are necessary. Only an analytic proposition is necessary in the sense that its negation is a contradiction in terms.[1]

To see what Kant means by regarding as necessary all *a priori* judgements, and not only the analytic ones, compare the synthetic *a priori* judgement 'Every change has a cause' with the synthetic *a posteriori* judgement 'Every man dies before the 300th year of his age'. In accepting that every change has a cause *we exclude the possibility* that any change is without a cause, even if in a particular case we cannot find it. In accepting that every man dies before he is 300 *we do not mean to exclude the possibility* of a man living longer than that, and are prepared to abandon our position if we meet such a man. Clearly the former proposition can be called necessary and universal in a sense in which the latter cannot.

Kant believes that necessity and strict universality, although not used in his definition of *a priori* judgements, are, jointly and separately, adequate tests of their *a priori* character: 'First, if we meet a proposition which in being thought is thought as having *necessity*, then it is a judgement *a priori*. Second: ... If a judgement is thought in strict universality, that is to say without admitting the possibility of an exception, then it is not derived from experience, but *a priori* valid.'[2]

The criteria of *a priori* character in a judgement are less clear than the definition of '*a priori* judgement'. It is very clear, however, that the necessity which is in all *a priori* judgements according to Kant is not the logical necessity of analytic ones. If it were Kant would have been guilty of a very elementary confusion. He would have been found defining synthetic *a priori*

1. This is obvious also, e.g. from *Pu. R.* 141 ff., B 189 ff.
2. *Pu. R.* 28, B 3.

propositions as logically necessary and as not logically necessary in the same sense of the term.

What makes all *a priori* propositions necessary, in the wider sense of the term, is their function in all our thinking about matters of fact – especially our scientific thinking. In what way, precisely, Kant thinks they are involved in or presupposed by our thinking cannot be shown in a few words, but it may be of use in giving some rough idea of the manner in which analytic and synthetic *a priori* propositions could be presupposed in our thought if we ask ourselves what would happen to our thinking if we denied these propositions. Let us first see what follows from the denial of an analytic proposition, say the proposition that every rainy day is wet. We should be committed to the proposition that some rainy days are not rainy and consequently to the statement that two contradictory propositions (which differ only in that the one denies what the other asserts) may both be true. This would deprive us of the possibility of consistent thought. More bluntly, we just could not think.

The consequences of the denial of a synthetic *a priori* proposition are less disastrous. To deny that every change is caused would be to deprive ourselves only of the possibility of using the concept 'cause' (defined as implying universal causation) which occurs in the proposition. But there are certain judgements about physical objects such that if they turned out to be synthetic *a priori* their denial would make impossible all commonsense thought about the external world and all scientific thought.

The synthetic *a priori* judgements which are presupposed by our thinking in a certain field need not be obvious to us and it may be difficult to make them so. We discover them only by looking for them in the permanent regions or features of our thinking. Such a search may, of course, miscarry. It may happen that what we regard as a permanent achievement of human thought, incapable of improvement, is merely transient. The supposed permanent presuppositions of thinking in the field in question would then have been shown to be relative only. One might indeed feel tempted to distinguish relative from

absolute synthetic *a priori* propositions or simply cease to
speak of the latter at all but always to specify the field in which
they are presupposed.

Kant himself does not make this distinction, since he believes
himself to have discovered all the absolute synthetic presuppositions of our thinking. They are, in particular, the presuppositions of arithmetic and Euclidean geometry, of Newtonian
physics, and, in a sense, of the traditional logic. Since he believed these fields of thought themselves to be ultimate and
permanent achievements of the human mind, he naturally
regarded their presuppositions as absolute.

In view of the great changes since Kant's time which have
taken place in all the subjects whose synthetic *a priori* judgements he tried to discover and to examine, one would hardly
expect to find that all of them are necessary to all thinking
about matters of fact. Later I shall draw attention to some of
them which are implicit in Euclidean geometry, but not in all
geometry, and in Newtonian physics, but not in all physics.

Kant further believed that his list of synthetic *a priori* judgements was complete in the sense that those he does not mention are deducible from those which he has listed. If not all of
his synthetic *a priori* judgements are absolute, if some are but
relative to changing subject matter, then Kant's claim to have
provided a complete system of these judgements cannot be
justified.

Kant spent much subtle thought and great labour on his
attempt to prove his system of these judgements complete.
For the purpose of our study here it will not be necessary to
deal with this aspect of his work at any length. Its interest is
almost wholly historical and its relevance to contemporary
philosophy slight.

There are, then, according to Kant, judgements which are
synthetic (i.e. their negations are not self-contradictory) and
a priori (i.e. they are logically independent of judgements describing sense-impressions). The objection that there cannot be
such judgements is based on a misunderstanding of the manner in which all *a priori* propositions are necessary. The minor

objection that Kant's notion of synthetic judgements is inadequate because it is defined by means of a spatial metaphor and for subject-predicate propositions only, has been answered by substituting for the metaphorical notion of 'containing' the notion of self-contradiction. And the latter is clear enough for our purposes even if, as I agree, there are purely logical problems connected with it on which unanimity of expert opinion has not yet been reached.

4. Sense, Understanding, Reason

The manner in which Kant addresses himself to the problem of synthetic *a priori* judgements depends, of course, on his general view of judging or, what to him is almost the same, thinking. One of his fundamental assumptions is that judging and perceiving are irreducibly different. In this he is opposed both to his rationalist predecessors, for whom perceiving was a kind of low-grade judging, and to his empiricist teachers, who were inclined to assimilate judging to perceiving. Kant expresses the sharp distinction between judging and perceiving as one between two distinct faculties of the mind: understanding and sense. 'By means of sense objects are *given* to us and sense alone provides us with *perceptions*; by means of the understanding objects are *thought* and from it there arise *concepts*.'[1]

Although quite different from it, judgement presupposes perception. As Kant puts it, 'directly or indirectly, all thinking must ultimately . . . refer to perceptions'.[2] This is not to say that all judgements are about perceptions, for clearly, analytic judgements, which merely elucidate the meaning of terms, are not. Yet the elucidation of terms is, as a rule, merely preparatory to their application to something perceived or perceivable. Definition is not normally an end in itself.

There can be no doubt that the judgements in which we apply general notions to what we perceive are of great impor-

1. *Pu. R.* 49, *B* 33.   2. *Loc. cit.*

tance in our thinking since they constitute the foundation of, and the evidence for, our commonsense knowledge of nature and our most subtle scientific theories. These judgements differ greatly (a) in the general notions which we are applying when we make them; (b) in the particulars to which these general notions are applied and, consequently, (c) in the manner in which the general notions refer to their particulars.

Consider the simple case of a judgement about a perceived particular, say 'This piece of paper is white.' Here the application of the general notion, 'white', to the particular hardly presents a problem. We have often perceived particulars which, although different in other respects, resemble each other in being white. To see this resemblance, to notice that they are all white, is to *abstract* the notion of whiteness from them. When, therefore, we judge of this particular that it is white, we are applying to this particular perceived piece of paper a notion abstracted from other particulars. We, so to speak, merely return to perception what we have taken from it.

In some slightly more complex cases we combine abstracted notions like 'white' with others, e.g. 'round' and 'hard', into a new notion 'white, round, and hard'. If the mode of combination is transparent enough we may, with some exaggeration, say again that in applying the compound general notion we have merely returned to perception what we have abstracted from it. Kant calls both the simple and compound abstractions from perception empirical or '*a posteriori* concepts'. The name fits well into his terminology since in applying *a posteriori* concepts we are making *a posteriori* judgements.

The doctrine that all, or at least all applicable, general notions are *a posteriori* concepts is one of the main tenets of empiricism. Whether true or not, it is certainly difficult to live up to this, as is shown by Hume's ingenious attempt to trace the notion of causal necessity entirely to sense-perception. We often judge that an event, say A (or of type A), causes another event, say B (or of type B). We do, in other words, apply the notion 'causes' to what we perceive. But do we also abstract this notion from our perceptions? True, we perceive that A is followed by B and that they are spatially and temporally near to each other. We may remember that A has so far always been followed by B and we may even have developed a habit of passing from the thought of A to the thought of B. All this, Kant holds, does not add up to the notion of causality, which is a kind of *necessary* connexion. It is, according to Kant, a general notion which, although applicable, is not abstracted from perception. It is an *a priori* concept.

If we employ such concepts, a question arises which does not arise in the case of *a posteriori* concepts, the question how they can possibly refer to anything. *A posteriori* concepts having been abstracted from perceptions are, so to speak, returned to them in judgement. But how and to what can *a priori* concepts refer? Among the many conceivable answers two are of special importance for understanding Kant's philosophy. It may first of all be that *a priori* concepts describe particulars which are not perceived or not given in the manner in which the instances of *a posteriori* concepts are given. We might call them *a priori* particulars. Kant, as we shall see, argues that space and time are such particulars. Their structure is described by synthetic *a priori* judgements, in which we apply the *a priori* concepts of geometry and arithmetic.

On the other hand it may be that the reference of *a priori* concepts differs in another way from the reference of the *a posteriori*. In applying *a posteriori* concepts we merely describe our perceptions, whereas perhaps the application of the other sort does something to them. This doing of something may, e.g., be a kind of ordering. Metaphorically speaking, by applying *a posteriori* concepts we are merely holding up a mirror to perception as it is given, or we illuminate an aspect of it; while by applying *a priori* concepts we transform our perceptions into a new product. If not taken too seriously, this metaphor may be of some help in understanding how concepts which are not abstracted from perceptions may yet refer to them.

Kant's excitement about this possibility is preserved for us in a letter (of 21 February 1772) to his friend and former pupil Marcus Herz. In the preface to the second edition of the

Critique of Pure Reason he compares his idea that in applying
a priori concepts to objects, the objects are made to conform
to the concepts instead of *vice versa*, with the fundamental
idea of Copernicus who instead of unprofitably assuming that
the firmament turned round the observer 'made the observer
turn round and kept the stars still'.[1]

It is now possible to explain in a preliminary way some of
Kant's terminology. Sense is the faculty of apprehending particulars which are given in space or time or both, and of
apprehending space and time themselves which are also particulars. The notions of space and time are for Kant not abstractions from perception but *a priori* particulars or 'pure
forms of perception'. The understanding is 'the faculty of cognition through concepts' which refer to sense-given particulars. These concepts are either *a posteriori*, that is to say abstracted from perceptions, or *a priori*, i.e. ordering them in a certain
manner.

We do not, however, exhaust our cognitive activities in
merely applying general concepts to perceived particulars.
There are other general notions which can easily be seen to
differ from those concepts, in that while they are clearly not
a posteriori (abstracted from perception) they are yet *not the same
sort of a priori* concept as, say, causality is. They differ in the
important respect that while they are like causality in not being
derived from perception, they are yet not, as causality is, applicable to perception. The sort of general notions which are thus
neither abstracted from perception nor applicable to it, Kant
designates 'Ideas'. The term is meant to remind us of the
Platonic Ideas – ideal standards which can be approximated,
but never fully conformed to by anything in the world of
sense. Merely to be inapplicable to perception, like, e.g. 'centaur', is not enough to make a general notion an Idea; it must
also be neither itself an abstraction from perception nor yet
anything composed of such abstractions. The faculty of employing Ideas is called reason in a narrow sense of the term.
(In a wider sense the term covers also the understanding and

1. *Pu. R.* 12, *B* xvi.

Def.
of
sense
+
understanding

I Ideas

in the widest meaning, found in the title of Kant's main work, it covers even sense, namely the pure forms of perception.)

The Ideas, then, are the notions which are farthest removed from perception. This does not, in any sense, make them unimportant. Indeed, Kant holds that God, freedom, and immortality are Ideas, and that by not understanding their function in thought we are condemning metaphysics to remain obscure and contradictory, 'the battlefield of endless quarrels'.

Kant distinguishes two uses of the Ideas, theoretical or speculative, and practical. Accordingly he distinguishes between theoretical or speculative reason and practical reason. In their theoretical function Ideas are employed in the service of scientific thought and all thought about matters of fact. In their practical function Ideas are involved in determining the will and in providing principles of moral conduct. In their theoretical function their remoteness from sense-perception is an ever-present source of danger – dangers of *fata morgana* in intellectual deserts and logical fallacies which pretend to satisfy deeply rooted human needs. In their practical function their remoteness from sense-perception and impulse is only to be expected and natural, since what ought to be the case often is not. In this way practical reason has a wider field than, or transcends, theoretical reason.

What has been said about the faculties of sense, understanding, and reason amounts to a classification, as yet unjustified, of particulars and general notions which together are the main constituents of judgements. To the *a priori* particulars, space and time, there corresponds pure sense; to the *a priori* concepts the pure understanding; to the Ideas, which, of course, are *a priori* notions, there corresponds in their theoretical use, pure theoretical, and in their practical use, pure practical reason.

In order to examine the nature of synthetic *a priori* judgements the critical philosophy must consider their possible *a priori* constituents. Its natural strategy was formulated in the introduction to the *Critique of Pure Reason* and was followed by Kant during many years of intense inquiry: it is to proceed from an examination of pure sense to that of the pure understanding, and hence to an examination of pure theoretical and pure practical reason. Towards the end of Kant's life the grand plan had to be somewhat modified as the result of what he believed to be discovery of new synthetic *a priori* principles implicit in aesthetic appreciation and teleological explanation.

CHAPTER TWO

SPACE, TIME, AND MATHEMATICS

1. Time and Space as *A Priori* Particulars

To state a synthetic *a priori* judgement is to apply an *a priori* concept, that is to say, one which is applicable to particulars although it has not been abstracted from sense-perception. One way, we have seen, of explaining how synthetic *a priori* judgements are possible would be to assume that they describe particulars which though found in our experience are yet not perceived by the senses. We know already that for Kant space and time are such *a priori* particulars and that the propositions of mathematics describe their structure.

That space and time are particulars, and not properties of or relations between particulars, was believed by Newton, whom Kant revered. Newton states that 'absolute, true and mathematical time, of itself, and from its own nature flows equally without relation to anything ...' and that 'absolute space, in its own nature, without relation to anything external, remains always similar and immovable'.[1] Against this Leibniz held that 'space ... is something *merely relative*, as time is ...', that it is 'an *order of coexistences* as time is an *order* of successions'. 'To take space' and, we may add, to take time, 'to be a substance, or at least an absolute being' he considers 'a fancy'.[2]

In the controversy between the Newtonians and the Leibnizians Kant sided with the former at least as early as 1768 when he published a brief paper whose title might be freely translated as 'The ultimate basis or ground of differences of direction in space'. There he considers, among other things, objects which are 'incongruent counterparts' one of the other, e.g. a

1. *Principia*, ed. Cajori, Berkeley, 1947, p. 7.
2. Third letter to Clarke, §§ 4, 5.

B

left- and a right-hand glove. The gloves are entirely similar yet
they cannot (even at different times) occupy the same space.
The difference between incongruent counterparts is for Kant
an example of those 'differences which refer solely to the
absolute and *original* space, because only through it the relationship of physical objects is possible . . .'[1] The difference, he
argues, cannot lie in the spatial relations of their parts, since
these relations are similar. It must therefore lie in their relation
to absolute space. The view that 'space' and 'time' designate
particulars, and not classes of relations between particulars, is
one which Kant never saw any reason to change.

The task of the *Critique of Pure Reason* in regard to space and
time is to prove not only their particularity but also their *a
priori* character. I must here try to express in a few lines how
Kant goes about this cardinal point of his argument. How
inadequate my words must be will be appreciated when I say
that Hans Vaihinger, one of the most acute and careful of
Kant's commentators, spends over one hundred explanatory
pages on this proof, none of which I consider wasted.

In order to prove that space is a particular, then, Kant considers the relation between *space* and *spaces*. Our imagination,
he believes, can picture only a single space, of which all spaces
which can be pictured are parts. Space is perceptual and is one
whole. Moreover, space can be split up into parts in a way in
which only particulars, and not also general notions, can be
divided. Space, therefore, is a particular. For the *a priori* character of space Kant offers mainly two proofs. He first argues that
in order to imagine two perceptions 'as being not only qualita-
tively different, but also external to and beside each other, . . .
space must already be presupposed'.[2] His second argument –
as I believe, the more convincing of the two – states that while
we cannot imagine there being no space, we can perfectly well
imagine space without anything in it. The point seems to be
that if space were an *a posteriori*, or abstracted, feature of perceptions we could imagine the perceptions without it. We cannot. We cannot, for example, imagine spatial and non-spatial

1. II, 383.   2. *Pu. R.* 52, *B* 38.

elephants in the way in which we can imagine elephants which
are grey and elephants which are not. If we perceive something
in space we cannot imagine it not in space. Therefore the notion of being in space, and space itself, are not abstracted but *a
priori*.[1] I cannot enter on the difficult and lengthy question as
to whether Kant has succeeded here. I can only assume he
has and continue with my exposition.

Satisfied that space is an *a priori* particular, Kant can now proceed to what he calls the 'transcendental exposition' of this
notion. By such an exposition he understands 'the explanation
of a notion as being a principle from which the possibility of
other *a priori* cognitions can be seen to follow'.[2] In this connexion we may note that Kant calls his whole philosophy transcendental because it is 'concerned not so much with objects,
as with the manner of our cognition of objects, in so far as it
is *a priori* possible'.[3] More precisely, a piece of knowledge is
transcendental if it is *a priori* and if by it we understand 'that
and why certain presentations (perceptions or concepts) are
only *a priori* applied or possible'.[4]

Since the discovery of Non-Euclidean geometries, we have
become familiar with the conception of *a* or *any* geometry; a
geometry being any system of implicit definitions applying to
entities postulated as conforming to the definitions. The question whether or not there are such entities is not raised and no
answer to it is expected from a geometry. Kant has of course
no conception of these developments. For him there is only
one geometry, the Euclidean, which he views as a body of synthetic *a priori* propositions about the structure of perceptual
space, for instance the proposition that space has only three
dimensions. This proposition is *a priori*. It is logically independent of any perceptual judgement. (That space is three-
dimensional does in particular not entail that any empirical
perception is or is not three-dimensional. The assumption of
space's being three-dimensional and all empirical perception
two-dimensional is not absurd.) And it is certainly synthetic,

1. *Pu. R.* 53 ff., *B* 38.   2. *Pu. R.* 54, *B* 40.
3. *Pu. R.* 43, *B* 25.   4. *Pu. R.* 78, *B* 80.

i.e. its negation is not contradictory; for the possibility of consistent many-dimensional geometries has been established for a long time.

Compare now 'Space is three-dimensional' with 'Chimborazo is white'. In the case of the latter judgement the synthetic connexion between its subject and its predicate is read off from a perception. In the case of the former judgement it is read off from an *a priori* particular. That the judgement is read off from a particular explains the synthetic character of the judgement; that the particular is *a priori* explains the judgement's *a priori* character.

Kant's treatment of time is similar to that of space. In order to show that time is a particular he especially argues that 'Different times are only parts of the same time'. In order to show that time is *a priori* he points out that we cannot imagine any perception which would not be in time, although we can imagine empty time.[1] Consequently, what has been said about the synthetic *a priori* judgement 'Space has only three dimensions' applies in a similar manner to 'Time has only one dimension'.

There are mathematical judgements which cannot with equal plausibility be regarded as having been read off immediately from space and time. A preliminary articulation of these particulars or, as Kant calls it, a construction may be required. Mathematics, he says, 'must have as its ground some pure perception in which it can present its concepts *in concreto* and yet *a priori*, that is to say, in which it can construct them'.[2] 'To construct a concept means: to present the perception which corresponds to it *a priori*.'[3]

The construction, or *a priori* presentation, of a Euclidean triangle is analogous to the drawing of a physical triangle on a blackboard. The construction, or *a priori* presentation, of the number Two is analogous to the successive putting of one physical thing to another. Geometrical concepts are constructed in space, arithmetical in time and space.

1. *Pu. R.* 57 ff., *B* 46 ff. 2. *Prol.* 281.
3. *Pu. R.* 469, *B* 741.

Only by introducing the notion of the *a priori* presentation of concepts in space and time does Kant explain the possibility of all the judgements of Euclidean geometry, arithmetic, and, as he insists, of the mathematical theory of motion. These synthetic *a priori* judgements are, he holds, possible because they describe the *a priori* particulars of space and time or the construction of concepts in them.

Towards the end of the *Critique of Pure Reason* Kant contrasts philosophy with mathematics by emphasizing again that only the latter can construct its concepts and thus, so to speak, provide objects for them. Therein lies, according to Kant, the reason why 'the mathematician by employing his method in philosophy can only produce so many houses of cards and why the philosopher by employing his method in mathematics can but stimulate idle talk ...'[1]

2. The Problem of the Reality of Space and Time

The permanent features of a changing thing or activity are often called its form. Since situation in space or in space and time are invariant features of perception Kant speaks of them as the forms of perception. The matter he takes to be the result of sensation, i.e. the result of our being affected by objects.[2] To use a very crude analogy, space and time are the spectacles through which our eyes are affected by objects. The spectacles are irremovable. Objects can be seen only through them. Objects, therefore, can never be seen as they are in themselves.

From the thesis that situation in space and time is not anything abstracted from perception, but something given *a priori*, Kant infers that space and time are contributed by the perceiving subject. It has often been pointed out that the argument from the *a priori* character of space and time to their subjectivity is not conclusive. It is always logically possible that what we perceive under the form of space and time is so

1. *Pu. R.* 477, *B* 755.　　　2. *Pu. R.* 50, *B* 34.

ordered independently of our perception. It is quite possible that what a person sees through his irremovable spectacles as, let us say, pink, is also pink in fact, and would be seen so even if *per impossibile* the spectacles were removed.

One can agree with Kant's view that the matter and form of perception are distinct, without sharing his view that the form is subjective. Thus even a realist, who believes that the thing he perceives exists just as he perceives it, could adopt the Kantian distinction without inconsistency. Moreover, he could hold with Kant that the matter cannot be perceived except under the form, because the separation of perceptions from their situation in space and time is only possible – as is, e.g., the separation of the shape and colour of perceived patches – in thought, but not in fact.

Whatever we may think of the validity of the inference to the subjectivity of a notion from its *a priori* character, Kant does hold that the *a priori* forms of perception are also subjective; and that we consequently cannot perceive the world as it is. We change it by perceiving it. This being so the question arises whether space and time, being subjective forms, are real or – what seems a philosophically preferable way to put it – in what sense they are real and in what sense they are not.

Space, it follows from the Kantian analysis, is empirically real; that is to say, it is real 'with respect to everything which can be given to us as an external object'. It is also transcendentally ideal; which means, in Kantian nomenclature, that 'with respect to things ... considered in themselves' space is not real.[1] Time, too, in which all perceptions are situated, is empirically real, that is to say it is real 'with respect to all objects which could ever be given to our senses' and it is transcendentally ideal. 'Once we abstract from the subjective conditions of perception it is nothing at all and cannot be attributed to the things in themselves.'[2]

Kant's transcendental idealism must be distinguished from Berkeley's idealism, the central doctrine of which is quite well expressed by the aphorism that to be is to be perceived. For

1. *Pu. R.* 56, *B* 44.   2. *Pu. R.* 61, *B* 44.

Berkeley the assumption of an unperceived existent is a contradiction in terms. Not so for Kant. What for him is a contradiction in terms is merely the assumption that an existent can be perceived as it is.

If space and time are subjective forms of perception then we must distinguish between things as they are in themselves and the world of appearances, a world moulded by the apprehending, i.e. the perceiving and thinking, subject. These appearances, as Kant points out, are not *mere* appearances. They are not illusions. A Kantian can distinguish just as a realist can between delusive and non-delusive perceptions, and by the same criteria.

3. On the Relation of Kant's Philosophy of Mathematics to Contemporary Theories

Before leaving Kant's account of space, time, and mathematics we may cast a brief glance on contemporary theories. The main issue is still the question whether the propositions of mathematics are analytic, as was believed by Leibniz, or synthetic, as was believed by Kant.

Bertrand Russell could, in his *Introduction to Mathematical Philosophy* which appeared in 1919, state with some justification that the whole trend of modern mathematics had been against the Kantian theory. At that time mathematical philosophy was dominated by his own important logical works, in particular by *Principia Mathematica* whose joint author he was with A. N. Whitehead. According to Russell there is no essential difference between the propositions of mathematics and those of logic, both of which he regards as being analytic and therefore not as being about any particular objects of any special kind. In order to prove his thesis he attempts to show that mathematics can be deduced from logic. In the system of *Principia Mathematica* this is achieved with the help of certain assumptions whose analytic character and logical status are highly dubious.

Mathematical logicians who believe with Russell in the analytic character of mathematics have for some time been trying to reconstruct the system of *Principia Mathematica*. Others do not think this possible. They believe that mathematical statements are statements about something – although not necessarily about Kantian space and time or constructions in them.

Thus Hilbert and his pupils distinguish between what they call formalized mathematical theories and meta-mathematics, i.e. the inquiry into the former. A formalized mathematical theory consists of (a) signs, which are analogous to the vocabulary of a language, but are considered in abstraction from their meaning; (b) rules for the combination of these signs into formulae, which are analogous to sentences; and (c) rules for the transformation of formulae into new formulae, a process analogous to deduction. The physical features of the formalized theory are considered irrelevant.

A formalized theory is thus a constructed particular which has a marked similarity to Kant's *a priori* constructions. Moreover, just as according to Kant the statements of mathematics are about something, namely space and time or constructions in them, so according to Hilbert meta-mathematical statements are about formalized theories. The similarity of Hilbert's view of arithmetic to that of Kant is especially close. 'Let us think', he says in one of his best-known papers,[1] 'of the nature and method of the ordinary finite theory of numbers', that is to say arithmetic without assumptions about infinite totalities. 'This theory can certainly be built solely through number-constructions by means of non-formalistic (*inhaltliche*) intuitive considerations.' This is a Kantian idea which is even, as it seems to me, deliberately formulated in Kantian language.

The difference is greater between Hilbert's and Kant's account of geometry. This is due to the fact, known to Hilbert but not to Kant, that while there is only one finite theory of numbers there are many geometries, among which Euclidean geometry is not necessarily the most useful for the description of the physical world.

1. 'On the Infinite', *Mathematische Annalen*, 1926, p. 171.

The second contemporary school of mathematical philosophy, which believes that mathematical judgements are not
analytic, is that of Brouwer, who explicitly appeals to Kant. In
a paper on 'Intuitionism and Formalism',[1] Brouwer says that
while he has abandoned the apriority of space he is adhering
the more resolutely to the apriority of time. He regards as the
fundamental phenomenon of mathematical thinking 'the intuition of the bare two-oneness. This intuition of two-oneness,
the basal intuition of mathematics, creates not only the numbers one and two, but also all finite ordinal numbers ...' It is
clear that this creative intuition is a near relative of the Kantian construction of numbers – *in concreto* and yet *a priori* –
in time.

Kant's doctrine of the subjective character of space and time
and consequently of things in themselves has little relevance
to philosophy of mathematics as such. If mathematical judgements are about space and time and constructions in them,
then it does not matter to the mathematician whether these
particulars have or have not their source in the percipient – so
long as they are the same for everybody.

For Kant's philosophy the doctrine is central and we must,
therefore, mention a serious difficulty in it which was expressed
as early as 1787 by F. H. Jacobi (in an essay *On the Transcendental Idealism* appended to a work on Hume), and was represented
to Kant by his disciple Beck in a letter written ten years later
(20 June 1797). Kant assumes without qualification that perception is in part caused by the action of things in themselves
on the perceiving self. Now causation, in the ordinary meaning
of the term, presupposes that cause and effect are located in
space and time, whereas according to Kant things in themselves are not so located. The assumption that the things in
themselves act upon the senses is thus contradictory.

The contradiction can be removed by interpreting the causal
relation between things in themselves and the perceiving self
as being different from causal relations between appearances or
by altogether abandoning Kant's causal theory of perception

1. *Bulletin of the Amer. Math. Soc.*, 1913, p. 85.

while keeping the rest of his system as far as possible intact. The former course is adopted by, among others, Dr Ewing in his Commentary on the *Critique of Pure Reason*, the latter by Leonard Nelson in his book *Über das sogenannte Erkenntnisproblem*.

CHAPTER THREE

THE SYSTEM OF *A PRIORI* CONCEPTS

1. Formal and Transcendental Logic

HAVING exhibited the two *a priori* forms of perception and explained the character – *a priori* and yet synthetic – of mathematical judgements, Kant has completed his theory of pure sense, 'Transcendental Aesthetic' as he calls it. In the next main division of the *Critique of Pure Reason*, 'Transcendental Logic', he sets himself three main tasks: first to separate out those *a priori* concepts which though not mathematical are, nevertheless, like, e.g., causality, applicable to perception, and to distinguish them from other types of concept; second to show how the proper application of such concepts leads to those synthetic *a priori* judgements which, he believes, are presupposed in commonsense and scientific thought about nature; and third to show how the improper application of *a priori* concepts and Ideas (i.e. general notions like moral freedom which are neither applicable to nor abstracted from perception) leads to certain far-reaching mistakes and confusions to which our human constitution makes us prone.

Kant explains his conception of transcendental logic by first considering the ordinary formal logic – that is to say the traditional Aristotelian formal logic of his day. Except for the one important fact that he considered this system to be the whole of logic, his views on its nature are entirely compatible with the results of the important modern development of the science after his death. Now, as in his day, the propositions of logic are regarded as *a priori* and as being about the form and not the content of their subject matter.

The difficulties involved in the notions of logical form and content are notorious; but it will suffice for our purposes here if we roughly define the form of a judgement simply as all those features of it which are relevant to the validity of a deductive inference in which it occurs as a premiss. Consider, for example, the inference from the premisses 'All men are mortal' and 'Socrates is a man' to the conclusion 'Socrates is mortal'. It makes no difference to the validity of this inference who draws it, whether its premisses are true or false, or what kind of objects they are about. It would still be valid if, e.g., one substituted 'immortal' for 'mortal' and 'unicorn' for 'man'.

What does matter, for the validity of the inference, is that it should conform to a general principle which can be formulated as follows: If falling under a general notion, say A, entails falling under another general notion, say B, and if an entity m falls under A, then it also falls under B – whatever A, B, and m are. The general notions may be *a priori* or *a posteriori* or without any application. The entity m may be an *a priori* particular (such as a Euclidean triangle or a moment of time), an *a posteriori* particular (such as a stone or an elephant) or, for that matter, an entity such as could not be given to human perception. The principles of formal logic are so general that they are indifferent to the intimate relationship in which according to Kant our thinking stands to perception. Any sort of thinking, even thinking which in no way depended on perceiving for its objects, would still conform to these principles.

Now Kant conceived the idea of a new science which like formal logic would be a body of *a priori* principles governing correct thinking. But it would differ from formal logic in containing the *a priori* principles which govern the application of *a priori* concepts. It is also conceived as being different from the *a priori* science of mathematics: for its principles do not describe the structure of the forms of perception. Briefly, the position is that if outside mathematics we do in fact apply *a priori* concepts, then there is room for this new *a priori* science. That we do apply such concepts and that causality is one of them is assumed by Kant in his introduction to the *Critique of Pure Reason* and is one of the theses which he hopes to establish.

In the Transcendental Aesthetic Kant sets out to show that

the notions of pure mathematics are *a priori* and how they can nevertheless refer to objects. In his Transcendental Logic he sets out to show that some non-mathematical concepts are *a priori* and how they can nevertheless refer to objects.[1] Just as he distinguishes between the *a priori* science of mathematics and the Transcendental Aesthetic which 'shows its possibility', so we should, strictly speaking, distinguish between the *a priori* science containing the principles for the application of *a priori* concepts and the Transcendental Logic which shows the possibility of that science. Kant does not give any name to the latter science. But it will turn out to be the *a priori* part of the natural sciences or rather of Newtonian physics.

It is a fundamental axiom of the Kantian philosophy that our thinking depends for its objects on perception. Only the principles of formal logic and our analytic judgements are unaffected by this dependence – apart from the fact that there would be no point in our analytic judgements if we did not also make synthetic ones. In all our synthetic judgements we apply concepts which refer to perception although the manner of this reference varies with different kinds of concept. We know that Kant is prepared to accept the empiricist account of the manner in which concepts refer to particulars only in the case of concepts which are abstracted from sense-perception. We also know his own account of the reference of mathematical concepts to space and time. As regards the manner in which, on Kant's principles, the other *a priori* concepts, e.g. causality, are applied, we know only that they must in some way refer to perception. The application of these concepts depends in Kant's words 'on the condition: that objects are given to us in perception, to which they could be applied'.[2]

Kant divides the Transcendental Logic in two parts: Transcendental Analytic and Transcendental Dialectic. The former deals with the application of *a priori* concepts in so far as it satisfies the fundamental condition of possible reference to perception. The latter deals with the improper and fallacious application of such concepts, which violates this condition, in

1. *Pu. R.* 78, *B* 81.   2. *Pu. R.* 81, *B* 87.

particular with their illusory application to things in themselves.

This division of the Transcendental Logic is analogous to a similar division of formal logic. The proper use of formal logic is analytical, its use as a negative test of factual truth. Its dialectical use consists in the improper employment of its principles as a means of the discovery of new facts. A biologist uses formal logic analytically if he uses it to test the consistency of his theory – which must be false if it is inconsistent, but need not be true if consistent. He uses it dialectically if he substitutes formal logic for factual inquiry. The distinction between the analytical use of formal logic and the dialectical remains valid in spite of the very considerable development of both techniques since Kant. Just as formal dialectic is concerned with whatever goes beyond the field of competence of formal logic, so Transcendental Dialectic deals with a similar transgression in the field of Transcendental Logic. Either transgression results in fallacy, illusion, and confusion.

The field of the pure understanding consists of (1) the non-mathematical *a priori concepts* and (2) the *a priori principles* whose statement involves the application of these concepts. The concepts may or may not be elementary. They are elementary if they are not deductions from or combinations of other *a priori* concepts. Kant believed it possible to draw a complete and detailed map of this province of thought. Towards the realization of this impressive design in logical geography the Transcendental Analytic is intended to provide an exact large-scale plan together with the instructions necessary for filling in all the detail. In its first part, the 'Analytic of Concepts', it undertakes to survey the whole field of elementary *a priori* concepts; in its second part, the 'Analytic of Principles', all the synthetic *a priori* judgements in which these concepts are applied.

2. The Method of Discovering the Concepts of the Pure Understanding

The first task of the Analytic is to establish a complete list of all the elementary non-mathematical but yet applicable *a priori* concepts or, as Kant calls them – for good reasons which will appear in the course of this argument – the 'Categories'. We can appreciate the difficulty of this undertaking and the philosophical daring behind it if we remember that the controversy about the *a priori* character of the single concept of causality is quite as much alive today as it was in the time of Hume. Kant, however, could go about to find all the Categories. He had, so he believed, a method. It is useful for the understanding and examination of Kant's position, to distinguish the more modest claim that he had a method from the larger one that it guaranteed complete success.

The Categories are not abstracted from perception. In order to discover them we must, therefore, examine thinking or judging or, what for Kant again amounts to the same thing, the application of concepts. Now whenever we apply a concept we unify or 'contract' many presentations, the latter being given, remembered and combined perceptual data. This unifying function of judgements and concepts is quite different from the passive apprehension which perception is. It is also different from the imaginative composition of a plurality of presentations into one. We need not know the mechanism of these processes in order to realize the difference between passively apprehending a red patch; unifying remembered and given perceptual data into the *concept* 'red patch'; and lastly, combining data of these and a multitude of other sorts into the kind of imaginative composition which we would call, say, a centaur, a limerick, or a piece of music.

Now this unification or contraction of presentations into concepts is involved in every judgement, even in perceptual judgements such as 'This seems heavy to me'. Yet, although even these judgements are, in virtue of their unifying function,

different from the perceptions which they record, they nevertheless contain only concepts which are abstracted from sense-
perceptions.[1]

From this examination of perceptual judgements, an examination which has led to the discovery of the unifying function
of concepts, but not yet to the discovery of a Category, we
must turn to judgements which are farther removed from
perception. These are *Erfahrungsurteile*, objective empirical
judgements, for example 'This stone is heavy'. The difference
between an objective empirical judgement and a perceptual or
subjective empirical judgement lies in the following features.
First, an objective empirical judgement refers to an object and
not merely to a subjective impression. Second, an objective
empirical judgement is, if true, true for everybody. It is not
qualified by some such clause as 'in my consciousness' or 'as
it seems to me' but is generally valid, i.e. valid for everybody,
in every consciousness or, in Kantian terms, 'in consciousness
in general'.

Having made clear the difference between perceptual and
objective empirical judgements Kant asks whence the latter
derive their objective reference and general validity. Certainly
not from perception, which is fully described by perceptual
judgements. But if objective reference is not abstracted from
perception then it must be an original contribution of the
objective empirical judgement. 'All our judgements are first
of all perceptual judgements: they have validity solely for us,
i.e. for our subjectivity, and only afterwards *do we give them* a
new reference, reference to an object, and want them also to be
valid for us at all times and equally so for everybody else...'[2]

Which factor in an objective empirical judgement, say, 'This
stone is heavy', confers objectivity and generality upon the
corresponding perceptual judgement, say, 'This seems to me a
heavy stone'? Not certainly, either of the concepts 'stone' and
'heavy' (more exactly 'stone-as-it-seems-to-me' and 'heavy-
as-it-seems-to-me'), which are both explicitly used in the perceptual judgement.

1. *Prol.* e.g. 298.   2. *Prol.* 298, my italics.

In order to answer this question we must remember that in Kant's view to judge is to apply concepts or to unify presentations. If the difference between the objective judgement and the corresponding perceptual one does not lie in the application of the concepts 'stone' and 'heavy', then it must lie in the manner in which the objective judgement *further* unifies the presentations which are already unified in these concepts. It must, in other words, be found in the application of a further concept which is not used in the perceptual judgement. 'If we resolve all our synthetic judgements, in so far as they are objectively valid, then we find that they never consist of mere perceptions ... but that they would be impossible, had there not been added a pure concept of the understanding to the concepts which were abstracted from perception.'[1] Where now, in the objective empirical judgement, are we to look for the *a priori* concept, the pure concept of the understanding which confers objectivity?

In every judgement we can distinguish two aspects: (a) the application of specific concepts; and (b) the manner of their connexion in the judgement, the latter being the logical form of the judgement. Now Kant argues that if what confers objectivity and generality on the objective empirical judgement is not to be (and it obviously cannot be) identified with its specific concepts, then it must be an *a priori* concept embodied in the form of the objective empirical judgement; and there will then be one elementary *a priori* concept or Category for each of the different ways in which objective empirical judgements confer objectivity and generality on the corresponding perceptual judgements.

It comes to this: if we can list all the forms of objective empirical judgement that are possible we can produce a complete list of the Categories. So Kant 'has found a clue', as he himself puts it; for he believed that the list had on the whole already been provided. The work of the traditional logicians here needed only some slight modification. The thesis that to each of the different logical forms there corresponds one Cate-

1. *Prol.* 302.

gory, and conversely, to every different Category one logical form, is in the words of Kant 'the clue for the discovery of all pure concepts of the understanding'.

Before turning to the use which Kant makes of this clue it is well to pause for a deep breath and to consider two assumptions he is making in this ingenious argument. The first is that to list all the possible logical forms of objective empirical judgement is a possible task, which is highly doubtful. Indeed his own list is mistaken. He considers, for example, that there is only one form of hypothetical or 'if – then' judgement. We know now, as indeed the Stoics knew,[1] that hypothetical judgements have a grammatical similarity which disguises fundamental logical differences amongst them.

The second assumption is that no new *a priori* concepts can be formed which would unify presentations in a new manner. There are such concepts. One which comes to mind at once as falling outside the Kantian scheme of Categories would be Whitehead's concept of four-dimensional events.[2] Here is a concept to apply which is to unify presentations in the manner exemplified in those objective empirical judgements which are found in relativity-physics.

That he should make the first of these assumptions so easily shows Kant's dependence on the traditional logic. This frequently comes to the surface in his writings, for example in the often quoted statement[3] that logic appears to be a science which to all intents is 'closed and completed'. The second assumption shows his dependence on Newton. He believed that objective empirical judgements could not be incompatible with the principles of Newton's physics.[4] It is, I believe, no overstatement of Kant's twofold dependence on Aristotle's logic and Newtonian science, if we describe his attempt at the discovery of all the Categories as an argument to the effect that the logical forms of traditional logic embody all *a priori* concepts of Newton's physics, which for him was natural science.

1. See, e.g., Bochenski, *Ancient Logic*, Amsterdam, 1951.
2. See, e.g., his *Concept of Nature*, Cambridge, 1930.
3. *Pu. R.* 7, *B* VIII.   4. *Pu. R.* 10, *B* XII, *Prol.* 295, etc.

All this is not to deny the importance of Kant's method for the discovery of *a priori* concepts. Its essence, as I see it, lies in the distinction between objective empirical and corresponding perceptual judgements, and in the examination of how the former confer objective reference and general validity on the latter. This is based on the realization that to apply concepts is to unify presentations.

3. From the Logical Forms of Judgement to the Categories

Without discussing Kant's differences from the traditional classification of the logical forms of judgement I propose here just to set down his own and comment briefly on it. To Kant it seemed final, and he employed it in fields of thought which lie far beyond the theory of knowledge, for example in his moral philosophy, his philosophy of purpose, and even his philosophy of religion.

(1) According to what is called its *quantity* every judgement is, in its form, either universal as in 'All men are mortal'; particular as in 'Some men are mortal'; or singular as in 'Socrates is mortal'.

(2) According to what is called its *quality* every judgement is either affirmative in form, e.g. 'All men are mortal'; or negative, e.g. 'It is not the case that Socrates is mortal'; or limitative (infinite), e.g. '(it is the case that) Socrates is not-mortal'. The distinction between negative and limitative is explained by means of another distinction, namely that between a positive concept and its complement, e.g. 'mortal' and 'not-mortal', 'green' and 'not-green'. In a negative judgement we deny that a thing or a class of things falls under a certain positive concept, while in a limiting judgement we affirm that it falls under the complement of such a concept. From the point of view of formal logic the difference between these ways of judging is considered as irrelevant.[1]

1. *Pu. R.* 88, *B* 97, *Logic, IX,* 104.

(3) According to what is called its *relation* every judgement is either categorical such as 'Socrates is a man'; or hypothetical such as 'If there exists a perfect justice then the persistently wicked will be punished'; or disjunctive such as 'The world exists either through blind chance or through inner necessity or through an external cause'. In a hypothetical and in a disjunctive judgement, but not also in a categorical one, we assert a relationship between propositions. In a disjunctive judgement we assert of two or more propositions that they are mutually exclusive and jointly exhaustive of all possibilities. In his *Logic*[1] Kant explicitly rejects the view of some logicians who 'believe that the hypothetical and the disjunctive judgements are nothing but various disguises of categorical ones and therefore without exception reducible to the latter'. It is regrettable that in his fundamental distinction between analytic and synthetic judgements he neglects the impossibility of such reduction.

(4) According to what is called its *modality* every judgement is either problematic in form, i.e. is logically possible; or assertoric, i.e. is true or can be correctly asserted; or it is apodictic, i.e. is necessary or can be asserted on *a priori* grounds. That the moon is made of green cheese is logically possible: it can be supposed, e.g., by a teacher of logic explaining the nature of deductive inference and using it as a premiss in an example. That iron is magnetic is true: it can be correctly asserted. That $2 + 2 = 4$ is necessary: it can be asserted on *a priori* grounds.

Having given reasons in the preceding sections for thinking Kant's belief mistaken that he had discovered the complete list of all logical forms of judgement, I need not criticize it in detail. Every logic text-book which takes notice of the development of the subject in the last hundred years does so implicitly; and, at times, explicitly. But only a comparatively minor part of the critical philosophy, although one that was very dear to him, depends on Kant's formal logic.

Before tracing the route which leads from the list of the twelve forms of judgement to the twelve Categories we may

1. *IX*, 109.

note that the so-called subjective empirical or perceptual judgements do not exhibit all the listed logical forms. As mere records of perception they certainly cannot be universal, negative, hypothetical, or problematic. This, of course, conforms to Kant's view, a view expressed most clearly in the *Prolegomena*, that the Categories which are embodied in the logical forms of judgement are not applied in merely perceptual judgements.

Perceptual judgements 'merely express a relation of two impressions to the same subject ...'[1] They are so close to perception that they hardly deserve the name of 'judgement'. This is obscured by the fact that if we wish to convey such a record of our perceptions we can often do so only by modifying and adapting the expressions we use for making objective empirical judgements. Thus we convey a subjective heavy-stone-like-impression by saying 'This seems to me a heavy stone' or 'This is a heavy stone – as it seems to me'. We use the clause 'it seems to me' in order, so to speak, to cross out the characteristics which the objective empirical judgement adds to perception.

In an objective empirical judgement, say 'This stone is heavy', we unify presentations by means of explicitly used concepts and the Category embodied in its logical form. Within this unification or synthesis Kant distinguishes the following elements. First of all, there must be given a manifold of presentations, i.e. perceived, remembered, and imagined data: for without a manifold to unify there could be no synthesis. Secondly, these presentations must be suitably collected by 'the imagination, a blind though indispensable function of the mind ...'[2] By the application of the concepts ('stone', 'heavy', *and* the Category) this collection is, thirdly, given necessary synthetic unity, that is to say, objective reference.

If we wish to isolate the Category from the other concepts which are applied in an objective empirical judgement, then we must consider the unification of those presentations only which are *a priori*, that is to say of the manifold of the structural

1. *Prol.* 299.   2. *Pu. R.* 91, *B* 103.

elements of space and time. This pure synthesis has again three aspects: the manifold of pure perception, the synthesis of the manifold by the imagination, and the conferment upon it of necessary synthetic unity or objective reference.

By unifying only the manifold of pure perception through the application of a Category we do not, of course, confer synthetic unity or objectivity on subjective impressions such as stone- and heaviness-impressions, but we confer it on an otherwise undetermined object – an object as such. What distinguishes different public objects from each other is thus not the applicability to them of the Category but the applicability to them of *a posteriori* concepts unifying presentations in space and time. The Category itself applies to any object whatsoever. (Concepts which apply to any object whatsoever were called 'categories' by Aristotle, which explains Kant's adoption of the term for the elementary concepts of the pure understanding.)

To apply a Category is, thus, to confer objective reference by unifying a manifold of pure perception. It is impossible to confer objectivity by a judgement unless the bearer of this objectivity, the object as opposed to a mere collection of subjective impressions, is produced in perception. Unless we confer objectivity by applying a Category there is no object in perception. Unless we produce an object in perception by unifying a pure manifold there is no characteristic of objectivity. More than that: the production of the object in perception and the application of a Category are two aspects of the same process.

This thesis, which forms the corner-stone of the Transcendental Analytic, Kant expresses as follows: 'The same function which *in a judgement* gives unity to the various presentations, also gives unity to the mere synthesis of various presentations *in a perception* which, generally expressed, is called "the pure concept of the understanding".'[1] A Category refers to its bearer because in being applied it produces it.

I shall not try to show in detail how Kant extracts a Category

1. *Pu. R.* 92, *B* 105.

from each of the different logical forms of judgement or how in this manner he derives his allegedly complete table of twelve Categories. The argument, it seems to me, is very much like that of a mathematician who, starting from premisses which have already been somewhat adjusted, desires very strongly to arrive at certain, to him, highly important conclusions, and who, in his very understandable eagerness, tends to forget some of the mathematical proprieties.

The following is but a crude outline, indeed almost a carica-ture, of Kant's procedure; and yet it fits his derivation of *some* of his Categories fairly well. To derive the Category em-bodied in a logical form, take any objective empirical judge-ment of this form and find the concept, the omission of whose application will turn the given judgement into a merely per-ceptual one. Since every objective empirical judgement has, as regards its form, quantity, quality, relation, and modality, there must be four concepts which will have the above effect. More crudely still, the 'equation': objective empirical judge-ment O minus Category X = a perceptual judgement, has four different solutions for any given O and twelve for all possible O's.

For example, by subtracting 'This is a substance with acci-dental properties' from 'This stone is heavy' or 'This is a heavy stone' we get the perceptual judgement 'This seems a heavy stone to me'. Therefore the Category embodied in the given and every other categorical judgement is 'substance-and-accident'. Again by subtracting 'This is an instance of a cause-effect relation' from 'If the sun shines then the stone becomes necessarily warm' we get 'First the sun shines on the stone and then it becomes warm – it seems to me'. Therefore the Category embodied in the given and any other hypotheti-cal judgement is that of causality.

I must desist from this crude exegetical game, and not even try to refine it to the high degree of subtlety which would do justice to a Kantian argument. For, however subtly derived, Kant's allegedly complete derivation of the table of Categories is incomplete and therefore incorrect. But I must at least set

The Categories

down his famous table of Categories with the corresponding logical forms. (1) *Categories of quantity*: to universal judgements corresponds the Category of unity; to particular judgements that of plurality; to singular judgements that of totality. (2) *Categories of quality*: to affirmative judgements corresponds the Category of reality; to negative judgements that of negation; to limitative judgements that of limitation. (3) *Categories of relation*: to categorical judgements corresponds the Category of substance-and-accident; to hypothetical judgements that of causality and dependence; to disjunctive judgements that of community or interaction. (4) *Categories of modality*: to problematic judgements corresponds the Category of possibility – impossibility; to assertoric judgements that of existence and non-existence; to apodictic judgements that of necessity – contingency.[1]

'About this table of Categories some rather nice reflections are possible which perhaps might have considerable consequences regarding the scientific form of all theoretical knowledge (*Vernunfterkenntnisse*).' One of them draws attention to the fact that the Categories of every class are three in number and that 'the third Category always arises from a connexion of the second and the first of its class. Thus totality is nothing but plurality regarded as unity ...'[2] This 'rather nice reflection' has indeed not been without considerable consequences, among which the triadic progress from thesis and antithesis to synthesis in Hegel's *Science of Logic* is the best known.

4. The Need to Justify the Application of the Categories

Kant, we have seen, has offered a proof to the effect that in making objective empirical judgements we apply elementary *a priori* concepts or Categories; that these Categories are twelve in number and that each of them is derived from one class of judgement, being embodied in its logical form. I take the view,

1. *Pu. R.* 93, B 106. 2. *Pu. R.* 95, B 110.

here, that even if his proof of the complete list of Categories was not successful he may still claim to have established that we do apply Categories in making objective empirical judgements. This is an important fact about our thinking which Kant's empiricist predecessors did not or would not see.

Yet the fact of our using Categories does not by itself imply that we have a 'right' to use them, since it may well be that we thereby in some sense misrepresent reality. This possibility cannot be *a limine* excluded, and there is indeed no lack of philosophers who consider judgements implying the alleged existence of substances or causal relations as false.

Thus there arises the problem of going beyond the fact of our use of the Categories and of proving the validity of this use or its rightfulness. This proof, in order to be valid, would have to show that without the Categories the experience of objects, i.e. objective experience (*Erfahrung*) as opposed to the mere occurrence of impressions, would be impossible. Kant calls this proof 'the Transcendental Deduction of the Categories': 'Transcendental' because it is directed not to a certain field of empirical knowledge, but towards a necessary condition of all such knowledge; 'deduction' because it, so to speak, establishes a right rather than a fact and because the term was used in this, now obsolete, sense by eighteenth-century jurists.

One of the most sympathetic and careful commentators on the *Critique of Pure Reason* (Professor Paton in his *Kant's Metaphysic of Experience*) compares the attempt to master the twistings and windings of this 'deduction' to the crossing of the Great Arabian desert. This is the task now before us. For our part, however, we must decline the hazards as well as sacrifice the rewards of a slow journey through difficult and austerely beautiful country and be well content if our quick flight over it permits us at least to descry, in its main outlines, the path the thinker followed.

Before considering the strategy and tactics of Kant's 'transcendental' argument it will be useful to glance back to another transcendental deduction which he has already given, namely that of the notions of space and time. That had been produced 'with small labour', Kant informs us, it consisting mainly in the demonstration that 'since only by means of such pure forms of sense can a thing appear to us, i.e. become an object of empirical perception, space and time are pure perceptions which contain *a priori* the condition of the possibility of appearances . . .'[1] As there can be no objective experience without perception, space and time as the necessary conditions of perception are also the necessary conditions of objective experience.

As regards the possibility of our having objective *experience*, it is by no means obvious that the application of the Categories (or of Categories) is a condition as clearly necessary for it as space and time have been seen to be. It has been shown that without the application of Categories there could be no objective empirical *judgements*. But, though objective experience cannot be had without perception, we can and do have such experience without passing objective empirical judgements. I cannot be confronted with a house or eat my dinner without perception and thus without its necessary conditions, space and time. But I can experience these objects without judging that they are a house or food.

In order to show that the Categories are as necessary as the forms of perception, if we are even to have experience of objects, we must inquire more deeply into the relation between perception and thinking and into the way in which the objects of experience are constituted.

It is clear enough that we do not come to know an object of experience, say a particular elephant, by merely forming the concept of an elephant: for we may form concepts which do not apply to anything in our experience. 'Thoughts without content' (that is to say concepts which cannot be applied to anything perceivable) 'are empty', says Kant.[2] It is equally clear that we cannot know an object of experience if it is unthinkable, i.e. if it cannot be judged to fall under any concept. So he adds, 'Perceptions without concepts are blind'.[3] No object of

1. *Pu. R.* 102, *B* 121.   2. *Pu. R.* 75, *B* 75.
3. *Pu. R. loc. cit.*

experience is possible if it be either unperceivable or unthinkable.

There are then two kinds of necessary conditions of all objective experience: on the one hand conditions necessary if objects are to be perceivable, on the other hand conditions necessary if they are to be thinkable. They must be both. 'The Transcendental Deduction of *a priori* concepts has, therefore, a principle, towards which the whole inquiry has to be directed, namely this: that they must be recognized as conditions *a priori* of the possibility of objective experience (be it of the perception which is encountered in it, or of the thought).'[1] If the applicability of the Categories is a necessary condition of objective experience, then it will be a condition of the second kind – a condition of the thought.

The problem of the Transcendental Deduction of the Categories has thus gradually become clear. In its first and almost metaphorical formulation, it appeared as the task of proving that their application is rightful. It was next formulated as the task of showing that the applicability of the Categories is a necessary condition of objective experience. In its final form the problem is to demonstrate that applicability of the Categories is a necessary condition of any experience of objects *in so far as they are thinkable*. We are therefore committed to an inquiry into the nature of thinking. And whatever more it may be, thinking, as we shall see presently, is at least connecting.

5. Thinking as Connecting

A manifold of presentations might conceivably be no more than a stream of impressions lacking all connexion. It may on the other hand have some unity. If we ascribe unity to a manifold we ascribe to it a characteristic which is quite different from any of its other features, for example the colours or noises which it contains. So much, I think, would be agreed on almost any view of perception and thinking.

1. *Pu. R.* 105, *B* 126.

According to Kant the connectedness or unity of a manifold is the result of a connexion or unification, while its other characteristics are merely perceived. Since of the two elements of cognition, sense and understanding, he conceives the former as an ability passively to receive impressions, the unity of the manifold must be the unifying work of the active understanding. In his own words: 'All connexion whether or not we become conscious of it . . . is an act of the understanding which we might call by the general name of *synthesis* in order to indicate thereby at the same time that we cannot represent to ourselves as connected in the manifold anything which we have not, ourselves, previously connected . . .'[1] 'The notion of connexion involves besides the notions of the manifold and of its synthesis the notion of its unity. Connexion is the representation of the *synthetic* unity of the manifold.'[2]

Kant's language in the quoted passages is that of introspective psychology describing processes as they follow each other in time. His point, however, is to analyse the structure of a connected manifold by distinguishing its characteristics and exhibiting their logical relations. Thus, in particular, the three notions involved in the synthetic unity of the manifold are not to be understood as different stages in a temporal development. The use of the language of introspective psychology in the Transcendental Logic, which was to be concerned with the possibility of objective experience and not with its natural history, might easily lead to a confusion of its subject matter with that of psychology. Against such confusion Kant issues frequent and forceful warnings.

The synthetic unity of a manifold must be distinguished from the Category of unity. If we state that a manifold has unity in the sense of the Category we state that a specific concept, the Category of unity, is applicable to it. If on the other hand we state that a manifold has synthetic unity we merely state that it is a possible foundation for the application of this or any other Category. The synthetic unity of a manifold is a necessary condition for the application of Categories but not

1. *Pu. R.* 107, *B* 130.   2. *Pu. R. loc. cit.*

itself a Category. A manifold without synthetic unity might be perceivable but could not be thinkable – at least not in objective empirical judgements.

If a manifold has synthetic unity, which is due to its unification by the understanding, then it must be thinkable by the *same subject* to which the unified perceptions are given. Synthetic unity of a manifold entails the unity of a thinking and perceiving subject, more precisely the unity of thinking and perceiving in a subject. For this unity it is not necessary that I should permanently think about my presentations. Nor is it necessary that when I think about them I should be aware of *my* thinking and *my* presentations. All that is required for the unity of myself in thought and perception is the *possibility* of this self-consciousness.

'The *I think* must be *capable* of accompanying all my presentations; otherwise something would be presented to me which could not be thought at all, which means no less than: the presentation would be either impossible, or at least nothing to me. .... Consequently every manifold of perception has a necessary relation to the *I think*, in the same subject in which the manifold is found.'[1]

The relation between the subject and the manifold of presentations which we express by saying that the *I think* must be capable of accompanying them, Kant calls 'pure apperception' or also 'the original apperception' in order to contrast it with 'apperception' in the sense of Leibniz and his school. According to Leibniz (e.g. *Principles of Nature and Grace Founded on Reason*, ed. Latta, p. 411), 'it is well to make distinction between *perception*, which is the inner state of the monad representing outer things, and *apperception*, which is *consciousness* or the reflective knowledge of this inner state, and which is not given to all souls or to the same souls at all times'.

Kant calls his notion 'pure' apperception because the necessary relation between the synthetic unity of the manifold and the *I think* is different from empirical apperception, which is the contingent association of self-awareness with other presenta-

1. *Pu. R.* 108, *B* 131.

tions. If pure apperception is given to 'a soul' at all, then it is given to it at all times, whereas empirical apperception, being an event in time, may be absent at some times and present at others.

Kant calls his notion also the 'original' apperception because it is that element in self-consciousness which while unifying presentations cannot itself be unified with other presentations in the same manner. The unity of the pure or original apperception Kant calls the 'transcendental' unity of apperception or self-consciousness, and thereby anticipates the role of the pure apperception in justifying the applicability of the Categories as a necessary condition of objective experience.

The terms 'synthetic unity of the manifold', 'pure and original apperception', 'transcendental unity of self-consciousness' are most certainly not ordinary terms of ordinary language, and Kant might have possibly invented a less forbidding terminology. On the other hand by using technical terms he does draw attention to important aspects of a subject which the language of polite conversation and *belles lettres* would probably merely adorn but not illuminate.

If we tried to express Kant's distinctions roughly in more ordinary terms we might say that a manifold of presentations may or may not be an *it* which can carry the burden of properties and relations. (In the latter case there is synthetic unity in the manifold.) There can be no *it* unless there is an *I* which could be aware of *it* and thereby of itself. (The possibility of this relation between *I* and *it* is the pure or original apperception.)

The transcendental unity of pure apperception is a necessary condition of objective experience (*Erfahrung*) and of objective cognition or knowledge (*Erkenntnis*) since without it no object would be thinkable. It is the form of the understanding in the same sense in which space is the form of outer perception. It might perhaps seem for a moment that mathematical knowledge, the object of which is the structure of space and time apart from their contents, does not 'stand under' the unity of pure apperception. This, however, is not so: 'for in order to know anything in space, for instance a line, I must *draw* it and in this manner synthetically produce a determinate connexion of the given manifold, so that the unity of this action is at the same time the unity of consciousness (in the concept of a line) through which alone an object (a determinate space) is known'.[1]

Kant's discussion of the relationship between the unity of objects and pure self-consciousness has deepened our understanding of the mutual interdependence of perceiving and thinking. There are objects of experience which we perceive and – by applying concepts to them – think. The knowledge of such objects presupposes both, the forms of perception, i.e. space and time, *and* the form of the understanding, i.e. the unity of pure apperception or self-consciousness.

Moreover – and this is the most important new result – the mere perception of a determinate object, i.e. one which is not but could be judged to be the bearer of concepts, presupposes the synthetic unity of the object, and consequently the unity of pure apperception. In other words even the mere perception of a determinate object must stand under the forms of perception and the form of the understanding. We knew that according to Kant there can be no thinking without perception. We know now that there can be no determinate or connected perception without thinking.

The human understanding does not produce the manifold. There might be, Kant supposes, an understanding, if one may use the word, through whose self-consciousness the manifold of perception would be given and not merely connected, but what it would be like we cannot possibly imagine. It is worth noting that the idea of a conceiving perception or perceiving conception was made the corner-stone of the philosophy of Fichte. Kant's opinion of Fichte's contribution could hardly have been lower. It is politely expressed in a letter to Fichte (of December 1797) in which Kant advises him 'not to look back ... to the thorny paths of scholastics' and to devote 'his excellent talent' to 'lively and popular presentations'. It is

1. *Pu. R.* 112, *B* 137.

expressed very impolitely indeed in other passages of Kant's writings.

6. The Legitimate and Illegitimate Use of the Categories

good summary

The unity of pure apperception (i.e. the possibility that a subject which is conscious of itself should be conscious of the presentations given to it) is a necessary condition of the synthetic unity of a given manifold. To say that a manifold has synthetic unity is to say that it is an object, or a possible bearer of concepts which are not merely descriptive of subjective impressions – a possible bearer of 'is-the-case' concepts rather than 'as-it-seems-to-me' concepts. 'The transcendental unity of apperception is that unity through which all the manifold which is given in perception is united into a concept of an object. It is therefore called *objective* . . .'[1]

The objective unity of pure apperception – which constitutes objects or in which objects are constituted – must be distinguished from the subjective unity of consciousness, for example in our noticing that certain perceptions happen to be together, follow each other, or are associated by us.

The aim of the Transcendental Deduction of the Categories is to show that the applicability of the Categories is a necessary condition of the experience of objects. So far, however, Kant has only argued that the synthetic unity of apperception is a necessary condition of the experience of objects. The next step of the Transcendental Deduction must, therefore, be an examination of the relation between these conditions of objective experience.

That we apply Categories Kant has shown, by comparing objective with corresponding subjective perceptual judgements, e.g. 'This seems a heavy stone to me' with 'this is a heavy stone'. The difference between an objective judgement and a subjective lies, according to him, in the fact that by assert-

1. *Pu. R.* 113, *B* 139.

ing the objective we apply, in addition to the concepts occurring in the subjective judgement, a Category or Categories embodied in the former's logical form. Objective empirical judgements, and consequently the application of the Categories, confer objectivity on subjective perceptual judgements and the manifold of presentations which they describe.

The unity of pure apperception is a necessary condition of the synthetic unity of a manifold and thus of the experience of objects or objective experience. Objective empirical judgements[1] realize this condition or, more precisely, declare that it is realized. By means of them, in particular by their logical function which is the application of Categories, 'the manifold of given perceptions is brought under one pure apperception (*eine Apperception überhaupt*)'.[2] The unity of pure apperception, the applicability of the Categories, the possible experience of  objects mutually imply each other: this, I believe, is the essence of the Transcendental Deduction.

Its influence, at least in so far as it tries to lay bare the relations between perceiving and thinking in a perceiving and thinking subject, can be felt in the farthest corners of the Kantian system. Two very important implications are pointed out by Kant in the course of the argument itself. They concern (a) the illegitimate use of the Categories and (b) the nature of the self.

In order to draw a firm line between the use and misuse of the Categories Kant again considers the notion of knowing an object. The knowledge of an object involves 'two elements: firstly the concept through which an object as such is thought (the Category), and secondly the perception in which it is given'.[3] To think an object is to judge without inconsistency that an objective concept, i.e. a concept which entails a Category, is applicable. We can think a house, a centaur, and

1. In the *Critique of Pure Reason* Kant uses the term 'judgement' instead of 'objective empirical judgement'; see *Pu. R.* 114, *B* 142, especially the example. In the *Prolegomena* 'judgement' covers both objective and subjective judgements.

2. *Pu. R.* 115, *B* 143.   3. *Pu. R.* 117, *B* 146.

C

an immortal soul in this manner: for 'being a house',
'being a centaur', 'being an immortal soul' entail 'being a
substance', and the judgements to the effect that these concepts are applicable, whether true or false, are internally consistent.

Knowledge of an object (more precisely the act of coming
to know an object: *erkennen*) involves perceiving it *and* judging,
or being in the position to judge, correctly, that it falls under
a concept which involves a Category. We can know a house,
but not a centaur. Neither can we know an immortal soul,
although, according to Kant, there may be good reasons for
thinking *that* there are immortal souls. These reasons, however, fall outside the field of theoretical reason.

'Now all perception which is possible for us is sense-perception (aesthetic), therefore the thinking of an object as such
by means of a pure concept of the understanding can become
knowledge only in so far as it refers to objects of the senses.
Sense-perception, however, is either pure perception (space and
time) or empirical perception of that which, by sensation, is
immediately presented in space and time as real.'[1] Not even
'mathematical concepts' taken by themselves are 'knowledge
except in so far as it is assumed that there are things, which can
be presented only according to the form of that pure sense-
perception. *Things in space and time* are only given in so far as
they are sense-perceptions (presentations accompanied by sensation).'[2]

The alleged application of Categories to objects which are
not given in perception can thus yield no knowledge. Any attempt of metaphysicians to achieve knowledge *in this manner* is
doomed to failure. Metaphysics *of this sort* is at most a universal disposition to theoretical hallucinations which must be
diagnosed and cured. Kant, here, anticipates the 'therapeutical'
attitude of logical positivism towards metaphysics. For him,
however, metaphysics is not wholly a collection of metaphysical illusions. His theory and therapy of those metaphysical
illusions and confusions which arise from the misuse of *a*

1. *Pu. R.* 117, *B* 146.　　　　2. *Pu. R. loc. cit., B* 146.

priori notions is contained in the Transcendental Dialectic which takes up well over a third part of the whole *Critique of Pure Reason*.

The second important corollary of the Transcendental Deduction concerns the nature of the self. In introspection I am at times aware of myself and perceive myself after the fashion of an object, that is to say under the form of time, though not of space, and under the unity of pure apperception. The experience of objects which must take place under the forms of perception and the understanding is not any experience of things in themselves. My empirical self must therefore be distinguished from my self in itself which is unknowable.

The self of pure apperception, the *I think* which must be *capable* of accompanying all my presentations, is not located in time. This we see clearly if we note that all the judgements about it contain a qualification of the form 'it is possible that' or 'it must be possible that' and no judgement of this kind refers to anything located in space or time. Of the self of pure apperception 'I am conscious not of how I appear to myself, or of how I am in myself but only *that* I am'.[1] The introspected or empirical self is knowable and known; the self of pure apperception is thinkable but cannot possibly be known.

That there should be an unknowable self seems nowadays perhaps a less strange doctrine than it seemed to Kant's contemporaries and even to Kant himself, who regards it as a paradox[2] which stands in need of being resolved. In any case, Kant's distinction between the pure self of which we only know *that* it is, and the empirical self which, with luck, we may sometimes know *as an object*, follows from the fundamental assumptions of his philosophy.

There have been many attempts to resolve the paradox by regarding it as a mistake. Schopenhauer, for example, distinguishes between the self as presentation which stands under the forms of perception and the understanding, and the self as will which is the self in itself. The self, and indeed for Schopen-

1. *Pu. R.* 123, *B* 157.　　　2. *Pu. R.* 120, *B* 152.

hauer everything given in perception, when divested of these forms, reveals itself as irrational force. This modification of Kant's philosophy by one who considered himself Kant's only true heir, turns the crowning achievement of the great European movement known as the enlightenment into one of the foundations of irrationalism. Indeed in some of Schopenhauer's pronouncements we can already hear the distant drum of twentieth-century savagery.

It is advisable here, before leaving the Transcendental Deduction of the Categories, to take full notice of a feeling of uneasiness, a suspicion of circularity in the whole argument, which may easily arise. We are supposing ourselves to be justifying the use of the Categories by demonstrating that the unity of pure apperception, the applicability of the Categories, and the possibility of objective experience mutually imply each other. It is in the nature of these implications that the root of the suspicion is found.

The implications are clearly not of the sort which obtains between two separate facts of experience such as the treatment of a certain illness with penicillin and the subsequent disappearance of the illness. Kant does not wish to prove that, as it happens, the unity of pure apperception, the applicability of the Categories, and the possibility of objective experience are in fact correlated. Neither does he wish to prove that in stating these implications one is formulating synthetic *a priori* propositions. This could be gathered from the circumstance alone that the sections of the *Critique of Pure Reason* which are supposed to contain all synthetic *a priori* principles do not list any of the implications as synthetic *a priori*.

We are thus left only with the possibility that the implications which the Transcendental Deduction wishes to establish are analytic propositions, i.e. propositions whose negations are self-contradictory. Kant's own words confirm this interpretation: 'The synthetic unity of consciousness is thus an objective condition of all knowledge ... which must be satisfied by every perception if it is to become *an object for me* because in any other manner and without this synthesis the manifold could not be united in one consciousness. This last proposition is, as has been said already, analytic.'[1]

According to Kant's own principles analytic propositions only elucidate the meaning of their terms and give no new factual information. Does the Transcendental Deduction, therefore, prove a mere tautology? The answer is that it does – in the same sense as the proof of any other analytic proposition. However, not every analytic proposition is trivial. Some certainly are. The implication, for example, that every father is male is both analytic and, I suppose, trivial. On the other hand the proposition that the axioms of arithmetic imply some complicated theorem, say, about prime numbers is analytic, but not trivial, because its truth is not obvious.

There is an additional reason why analytic propositions may be far from trivial, which becomes clear if we assume that a concept, say A, describes an important known fact and that somebody proves to us for the first time that A analytically implies B. Although this will not teach us a new fact, it may nevertheless teach us a great deal about the fact we knew already.

Kant's Transcendental Deduction, if correct, demonstrates analytic propositions which are by no means obvious. These propositions make us see new features of the well known fact that we experience objects, as also of the new fact, which Kant himself established, that we apply Categories.

1. *Pu. R.* 112, *B* 138.

CHAPTER FOUR

The System of Synthetic *A Priori* Principles

1. How the Categories are Applied

IN order to explain the nature and function of synthetic *a priori* judgements it was necessary for Kant to show that there are *a priori* particulars, namely space and time; that in making objective empirical judgements we apply Categories; and that we are justified in doing so. All this tells us much that is important about the constituent parts of synthetic *a priori* judgements, but not enough about the way in which they hang together.

Before considering the application of Categories in synthetic *a priori* judgements Kant considers in some detail the easier question of the application of *a posteriori* and of mathematical concepts to things given in perception. He holds that the application of these concepts to perception is not possible without the mediation of what he calls schemata. Thus before we can apply the concept 'dog' to Pluto we must, he believes, be capable of producing in our imagination a schematic representation of a dog. Similarly, before we can apply the concept 'geometrical circle' to a certain round saucer we must be capable of producing a schematic representation of a circle in our imagination.

The schema of a concept must be distinguished from the concept itself, from any instance of the concept, and from any picture of an instance. It is not even a specific schematic image. It is 'the presentation of a general procedure of the imagination in procuring an image for a concept'. It is 'a rule for the synthesis of the imagination'.[1] While the concept belongs to

1. *Pu. R.* 135, *B* 180, 81.

the understanding and its instance to perception, the schema has, so to speak, a foot in either domain. As *rules* for the production of images the schemata of 'dog' and 'geometrical circle' are linked to the understanding; as rules for the production of *images* they are linked to perception. It is in virtue of this twofold connexion that they themselves can link the concept 'dog' to Pluto and the geometrical circle to a particular round saucer.

In Kant's account of the schemata of *a posteriori* and mathematical concepts psychological and logical considerations are almost inextricably mixed and his psychological account of the production of schemata 'as an art hidden in the depths of the human soul' might easily obscure what is, I believe, his main point.[1]

In order to indicate, as briefly as may be, what this is we must distinguish between two kinds of rule governing the use of a concept. I shall call them respectively the 'referential' and the 'non-referential' rules. It is necessary that the referential rules be satisfied if the concept is to be applied correctly but not if it is employed in other ways, e.g. if it is being related to other concepts. For example, somebody, say, who is trying to learn English, may well know that 'being a dog' implies 'being a mammal', yet not know to what the terms 'dog' and 'mammal' refer. Such a person knows non-referential rules governing these concepts, their logical grammar, as it were, but not their referential rules.

Referential rules link concepts to perception and thus perform the function of Kant's schemata. Whatever else the addition of its schema to a concept may be for Kant, and whatever its psychological mechanism, it is at least the addition of the referential rules of a concept to its non-referential ones – an addition which makes the concept applicable.

Now as regards the Categories their links with perception, or in Kant's terminology their schemata, are less obvious. So far we know that the Categories are embodied in the logical forms of objective perceptual judgements and are applicable

1. *Pu. R. loc. cit.*

only to what is given in perception. Although this last condition is a general guide to the manner in which all Categories refer to perception, it does not by itself tell us the schemata or referential rules for each separate Category.

Kant calls the schemata of the Categories 'transcendental' in order to distinguish them from the schemata of *a posteriori* and of mathematical concepts. In his view their mechanism does not and indeed could not involve the production of schematic images of various species of things, such as dogs and circles, because the Categories refer to objects as such, and so to any and every object. We can procure schematic images for, say, 'dog' and 'circle', but not for 'object' as such.

The schema, and consequently the referential rules, of an *a posteriori* or mathematical concept determine the perceptual conditions under which it is applicable to manifolds which have the synthetic unity of *specific* objects such as dogs or saucers. Unschematized, or without their schemata, such concepts are mere logical shells without reference to perception. Of a Category, accordingly, the schema, and consequently the referential rules, determine the specific conditions under which it is applicable to *any* manifold which has the synthetic unity of anything whatever that is an object of experience. Now the only feature which is common to every object of experience, including the empirical self, is its being in time. The schema of a Category, therefore, determines the temporal conditions under which it is applicable to objects of experience in general. In Kant's words, 'the schemata (of the Categories) are therefore nothing but temporal determinations *a priori* in accordance with rules ...'[1] Without the schemata, or unschematized, the Categories have 'a merely logical significance of the mere unity of presentations, to which, however, there is given no object ...'[2]

Kant divides the schemata of the Categories into four groups. They correspond to the four divisions of the forms of judgement and of the Categories themselves. The Categories of quantity refer to the temporal series, those of quality to the

1. *Pu. R.* 138, *B* 184.   2. *Pu. R.* 139, *B* 186.

content of time, those of relation to temporal order and those of modality to the totality of time. The actual derivation of the schemata is, I believe, at least as artificial as that of the Categories. The important point, however, is not the completeness of the list but the thesis that Categories, in order to refer to perception, must be schematized. The statement of the rules which constitute the logical grammar of a Category must be supplemented by an indication of the perceptual conditions on which alone it can be applied to any possible object of experience.

I shall set down, now, the list of transcendental schemata without much comment. Kant himself says little enough in its justification. It must indeed have seemed too obvious for him to waste many words on it. Besides, the work of analysis necessary in order to ascertain what is required for transcendental schemata he considered 'dry and boring'. If he could have foreseen some of the explanations of the transcendental schematism, including perhaps the present, he might well have decided to say a little more about it.

(1) The schema of the Categories of quantity (unity, plurality, and totality) is number. An object which is given in perception is a quantity only if it can as a quantity be compared with other quantities, i.e. if it can be measured. Measurement implies the addition of units which is necessarily a succession in time. Number in Kant's words 'is nothing but the synthetic unity of a manifold in a homogeneous perception as such . . .'[1]

(2) The schema of the Categories of quality (reality, negation, limitation) is degree of intensity. Any empirical perception involves a sensation which must be capable of increasing or decreasing in intensity. The schematized Category of reality refers to any sensation in so far as it has some degree of intensity, while the schematized Category of negation refers to nothing, which is conceived as the degree zero of the intensity of any sensation as such.

(3) As regards the Categories of relation (substance, causality, and interaction), the schema or temporal determination of substance is permanence in time, that of causality is 'succession of

1. *Pu. R.* 137, *B* 182.

a manifold in so far as it is subject to a rule'.[1] While Kant
insists that the notion of causality is not equivalent to that of
regular succession, he holds that unless it implied this notion
it could not refer to anything in perception. The schema of the
Category of interaction 'of the substances in respect of their
accidents is the coexistence of the accidents of one substance
with those of the other in accordance with a general rule'.[2]
Regular coexistence of substances is again not supposed to
exhaust the notion of their interaction but to provide the necessary condition for applying the Category to what can be given
in perception.

(4) The schemata of the Categories of modality (possibility
– impossibility, existence – non-existence, necessity – contingency) are the following. The schema of possibility is possibility in time, not mere logical possibility. The schema of
existence (*Wirklichkeit*) is 'being at a certain time'. The schema
of necessity is 'the being of an object for all time'.[3]

The details of Kant's distinction between, on the one hand,
schematized and unschematized Categories and concepts in
general and, on the other, the psychological background
against which it is explained must not blind us to its importance. By separating the referential from the non-referential
rules which govern the employment of concepts, it clarifies the
function of conceptual thinking and its relation to the apprehension of particulars. It puts yet another obstacle in the way
of those of us who tend to forget that to think is, at least sometimes, to think about facts rather than thoughts; and, consequently, that language refers, at least sometimes, not to language but to extralinguistic entities. It is worth noting that
most contemporary logicians are convinced of the necessity
and fruitfulness of a distinction between a calculus and its
interpretation or between syntax and semantics.

To the critical philosophy as a whole the distinction between schematized and unschematized Categories is fundamental. Thus, as we shall see, Kant holds that reflection on our
moral experience leads unavoidably to the assumption of moral

1. *Pu. R.* 138, *B* 183.   2. *Pu. R. loc. cit.*   3. *Pu. R.* 138, *B* 184.

responsibility and consequently of moral freedom. This he conceives as a kind of causality which falls outside the order of fact, especially scientific fact. If the only possible causality were the schematized Category, according to which every event is causally determined, there would be no room for moral freedom. As it is we can believe without contradiction, and with good reason, that there is also an (unschematized) causality such as our moral experience demands. We can think that it exists but we can never know it. We cannot know it because we cannot know what is unperceivable.

2. The Subject Matter of (Theoretical) *A Priori* Judgements

Analytic judgements elucidate the meaning of their terms but do not go beyond them. Synthetic judgements on the other hand are about something which is, has been, or will be the case, or about something which ought to be the case. Judgements of the first type are theoretical, of the second practical. Here we are concerned only with the theoretical and can, therefore, without fear of misunderstanding speak of synthetic judgements instead of theoretical synthetic judgements, which circumlocution would, however, it is true, be more correct.

The relationship between the terms of any synthetic judgement depends not only on their meaning but on what is judged to be the case. In a synthetic *a posteriori* judgement such as 'Chimborazo is white' the relationship between the terms is read off from experience of a certain *a posteriori* particular. In a synthetic mathematical judgement such as '7 + 5 = 12' or 'every equiangular triangle is equilateral' it is, according to Kant, read off from an *a priori* construction in time or space. What, now, is the subject matter from which we read off synthetic *a priori* principles, as, with Kant, we shall be calling those synthetic *a priori* judgements in which a Category is applied?

The answer, to which almost all the preceding discussion has been leading up, is briefly: 'the possibility of objective

[handwritten: judgment why applies category]

[handwritten: synth apriori]

experience'.[1] To state such a principle is to state a condition without which objective experience would not be possible: for 'the conditions of the *possibility of objective experience* as such are at the same time conditions of the *possibility of the objects* of experience and have therefore objective validity in a synthetic judgement *a priori*'.[2]

Looking back, the following propositions stand out as milestones on the road which has led to this conclusion. Objective experience is describable by objective empirical judgements which differ from subjective or mere perceptual judgements only in that they involve the application of Categories. The application of a Category is legitimate only if it refers to the synthetic unity of a manifold of perception. Every Category is by its schema restricted to certain temporal conditions without which no object can be perceived and thought at the same time.

[handwritten: principles as rules for the objective use of Categories]

'The table of Categories quite naturally gives us a lead in constructing the table of principles, because the latter are after all nothing but rules for the objective use of the former.'[3] That is to say, unless a schematized Category is applicable to a manifold of perception the latter can have no synthetic unity and thus cannot be an object. It is only a new way of stating this necessary condition of objective experience (experience of an object) if we formulate the synthetic *a priori* principle, that every object must be a substratum of the Category. If the Category is a relation then we state the necessary condition of objective experience by saying that every object must stand in this relation to other objects.

For example, we know that unless the schematized Categories of quantity are applicable to a manifold of perception the manifold could have no synthetic unity and thus could not be an object. This necessary condition of objective experience is formulated in the principle that 'all perceptions are measurable [extensive] quantities',[4] i.e. they are comparable with others by means of a successive addition of some units. The

1. *Pu. R.* 144, *B* 195.   2. *Pu. R.* 145, *B* 197.
3. *Pu. R.* 147, *B* 200.   4. *Pu. R.* 148, *B* 202.

principle is synthetic because we may, I suppose, assume without self-contradiction that the perceptions of a mind which could only perceive and was incapable of thinking would not be so comparable. It is *a priori* since it entails no judgement (or negation of a judgement) describing a perception. Moreover, it also satisfies the criteria of generality and necessity which according to Kant are characteristic of all synthetic *a priori* judgements. In this connexion we must, of course, remember that Kant's notion of necessity is wider than the notion of logical necessity which covers analytic judgements only.

Kant gives in his Analytic of Principles detailed proofs of all the synthetic *a priori* principles which govern the application to objects or 'the objective use' of the Categories. The proofs (not all equally obvious and at times somewhat artificial) are symptomatic of a certain formalism which is characteristic of Kant's mentality, inclining him first to the conviction that the table of Categories is complete and then to the expectation that their schemata should lead to an equally complete table of the synthetic *a priori* principles of objective experience.

'The principles of possible objective experience are at the same time general laws of nature which can be known *a priori*'.[1] For clearly, if they express necessary conditions of objective experience they express *a fortiori* necessary conditions of natural science; since natural science describes, interprets, and predicts objective experience. These conditions have their source in the relation between thinking and perceiving. They are not abstracted from subjective experience, or from *a posteriori* principles, but are constitutive of objective experience. They are laws which the understanding 'prescribes to nature'.[2]

While the synthetic *a priori* principles are, according to Kant, the most general laws of nature, and although some of them can indeed be found among the propositions of Newtonian physics as unquestioned assumptions, Kant insists on a clear distinction being made between those laws of nature which are conditions of objective and, therefore, scientific experience, and those which are generalizations from objective experience.

1. *Prol.* 306.   2. *Prol.* 320.

Here, as in very many other philosophical issues debated between empiricists and rationalists, the Kantian position strikes
a balance between opposing parties. While empiricists hold
that all laws of nature are empirical generalizations of one kind
or another and rationalists are inclined to regard them as necessary in some sense which implies that they are not empirical,
Kant finds laws of both types in natural science.[1] Accordingly,
he distinguishes between a pure science of nature and an empirical. The empirical depends on the pure science for its
objectivity, and for its content on experiment and observation.
Synthetic *a priori* principles can be no substitute for work in
the laboratory, nor can work in the laboratory replace these
principles.

In the *Prolegomena* Kant divides the question how synthetic
judgements *a priori* are possible into four subordinate questions, namely: How is pure mathematics possible? How is pure
natural science possible? How is metaphysics in general possible? And, lastly, How is metaphysics as a science possible?
The first of these questions has been answered in the Transcendental Aesthetic and the third will be, in the main, answered
in the Transcendental Dialectic. The Transcendental Analytic
provides Kant's answer to the second question by showing
that a pure science of nature is possible as a body of synthetic
a priori principles which formulate necessary conditions of
any objective and so of any scientific experience.

The Transcendental Analytic gives also at least a partial
answer to Kant's fourth question, that about the possibility of
scientific metaphysics. Since metaphysical principles, as he conceives them, are all of the synthetic *a priori* judgements which
are not mathematical, the *a priori* principles of natural science
together with their logical consequences belong at the same
time to a scientific metaphysics, the 'metaphysic of nature', as
Kant calls it.

Besides the metaphysic of nature which contains the presuppositions of objective experience Kant recognizes a meta-

1. For a modern version of this issue see Kneale, *Probability and
Induction*, Oxford, 1949.

physic of morals which should contain the presuppositions of moral experience.[1] Whether the metaphysic of morals – which has practical but not also theoretical truth – is regarded as scientific by Kant is not quite clear. The question is hardly more than verbal. If the truth of the metaphysic of morals is 'scientific' then the metaphysic of nature is not the whole of scientific metaphysics.

It is convenient to distinguish between metaphysical presuppositions (of scientific, moral, and perhaps aesthetic experience) on the one hand, and absolute metaphysical propositions on the other. Some such distinction is made by Kant himself between metaphysics 'in its first part in which it occupies itself with concepts *a priori* to which the corresponding objects can be adequately given in experience ...' and metaphysics in its second part where this is not so.[2]

Just as Kant believes he has discovered all the Categories and their schemata, so he believes he has discovered the synthetic *a priori* principles of all possible objective experience. Discussion of Kant's table of Categories has revealed the possibility of alternatives to the Kantian system. It is seen, for example, in Whitehead's notion of a four-dimensional event. Another example would be some modern notion of probability. The schemata of the Categories, i.e. the perceptual conditions of their applicability, and consequently the *a priori* principles which state that they are necessary conditions of a type of objective experience, will also admit of alternatives. That the Kantian *a priori* principles of objective and scientific experience should admit of alternatives does not make their serious consideration the less worthwhile. There are two reasons for this. Firstly they constitute fundamental assumptions of a highly important stage in the development of scientific thought, and secondly they illustrate a method of inquiring into the general relationship between scientific propositions and philosophical assumptions.

1. *Gr.* 388, *Ab.* 2.   2. *Pu. R.* 13, *B* xix.

3. The Synthetic *A Priori* Principles of the Understanding

The synthetic *a priori* principles relate the Categories to the possibility of objective experience. We should, therefore, expect the principles to correspond to the Categories of quantity, of quality, of relation, and of modality. Although Kant does group the principles in this way he also, as we shall see, divides them differently, namely into two classes, in order to indicate their different functioning in scientific thought and in commonsense judgements about matter of fact.

To the Categories of quantity there correspond the *axioms of intuition*. Kant uses the term 'intuition' (*Anschauung*) almost synonymously with that of 'perception' (*Wahrnehmung*). The main differences are two; first, that 'intuition' covers not only perception but what would correspond to it in beings who apprehended particulars in a different manner from the human – a manner which on that account must be unknown to us; second, that 'perception', or rather its German equivalent, is always used in the sense of 'empirical perception'. It is, I believe, possible to make Kant's meaning clear using only the term 'perception', qualifying it, where necessary, as pure, empirical, or (thirdly and very rarely) non-human. In this way the misleading associations of the English word 'intuition' can be avoided and the axioms of intuition spoken of as axioms of pure and empirical perception.

'Their general principle' in Kant's words 'is: All perceptions are extensive magnitudes.'[1] The importance of the principle lies in the fact that it constitutes Kant's explanation of why mathematics is applicable to experience and why in particular mathematical physics is possible. For him the propositions of mathematics are not idealizations from experience but constitutive of it. In other words the reason why we can apply mathematics to experience is because its applicability is a necessary condition of there being experience at all. Kant does not mention any specific axioms of perception although he makes

1. *Pu. R.* 148, *B* 202.

it clear that the propositions of mathematics are not themselves the axioms in question. It would seem that these axioms themselves, as opposed to their principle, are the judgements which permit application of specific mathematical propositions to perception.

To the Categories of quality there correspond the *anticipations of empirical perception.* 'Their principle is: in all appearances the real which is an object of sensation has intensive magnitude, that is degree.'[1] This principle is less general than the previous one because it refers only to empirical and not also to pure perception. It is indeed obvious that the pure perception of, say, an *a priori* construction of a plane figure or of a succession of units has no degree of intensity although in actual fact it will always be accompanied by empirical perceptions involving sensations and therefore having intensity.

Kant's general principle of the anticipations of empirical perception shows us why mathematics is applicable in the measurement of sensation. Since, as Kant insists, the notion of a degree of intensity implies the possibility of its gradual and continuous increase from and decrease to zero, the mathematical theory of limits and the differential and integral calculus are particularly appropriate to the measurement of the intensity of sensation. Their use in this field has become current since the second half of the nineteenth century. Early examples of its fruitfulness are the Weber-Fechner law concerning the intensity of sensation and the first steps in the economic theory of marginal utility taken by Gossen and Jevons. It can, I believe, be said without much exaggeration that in formulating the principle of the anticipations Kant foresaw the necessity of a philosophical justification of all so-called psychometrics and some so-called econometrics and provided one such justification. This is not incompatible with his scepticism as to the possibility of ever applying mathematics to psychology and even chemistry.[2]

1. *Pu. R.* 151, *B* 207.
2. See *Metaphysical Foundations [Anfangsgründe] of Natural Science*, 1786.

The anticipations of empirical perception themselves must be distinguished from their general principle; also, on the other hand, from any specific application of mathematics to the measurement of the intensity of sensation. They are intended to consist, presumably, of the judgements which permit such application in particular cases. Kant is not very clear on the point, and it is in any case of but minor importance.

These two principles, that underlying the axioms of perception and that underlying the anticipations of empirical perception, are grouped together under the heading of the 'mathematical' principles of the pure understanding because they justify the application of mathematics. They are also the only principles which enable us *a priori* to predict perceivable properties of future perceptions: for while we cannot know what, say, our next perception will be like as a whole we do know that it will be an extensive magnitude and, if empirical, an intensive magnitude also. The principles which correspond to the next two groups of Categories, those of relation and of modality, principles which in distinction from the mathematical Kant calls 'dynamic', differ from the mathematical in two ways. They do not guarantee the applicability of mathematics to experience, and they do not explain the *a priori* predictability of the predictable perceptual features of experience.

We pass to the principle underlying the *analogies of objective experience*. These 'analogies' correspond to the Categories of relation. 'Their principle is:' to quote again, 'objective experience is possible only by means of the presentation of a necessary connexion of perceptions.'[1] The 'necessity' in question is, of course, not logical necessity. It refers to the synthetic unity of a given manifold of perceptions; the unity in virtue of which all of them are related to one object and consequently to each other. In this way the visual and tactual impressions of my fountain-pen are connected as belonging to the same object and, therefore, to each other. On the other hand the impressions in a dream may be unconnected, that is to say, a manifold without synthetic unity.

1. *Pu. R.* 158, *B* 218.

We saw in the Transcendental Deduction of the Categories that the synthetic unity of any given perceptual manifold is not a feature of the particular manifold but is a contribution from the understanding. It follows that the synthetic connexion of a perception with an object to which it belongs and with other perceptions belonging to this or another object cannot be perceived but can only be thought. It further follows that the principles governing this connexion will, so far as the prediction of perceptions is concerned, be, at the very best, guides or directives in our search for them without in any way ensuring the success of our search. Because they regulate our search for new perceptual facts Kant regards them as a species of 'regulative' principles and contrasts them with the 'constitutive' mathematical principles.[1]

The term 'analogy' Kant borrowed from mathematics, where it means proportion. A mathematical analogy, e.g. the equation $\frac{x}{a} = \frac{b}{c}$, tells us not only that a, b, c, stand in a certain relation to x but also gives us x. A philosophical analogy, more particularly an analogy of experience, tells us only that *there exists* an x which stands in a certain relation to given terms without, however, actually giving us the x. For example the principle of causality (one of the analogies) tells us only that for any given event *there exists* another event which is its cause. It cannot reveal the event. A philosophical analogy, as described by Kant, is indeed rather like the mathematician's 'existence theorems', that is to say, theorems which state that a term stands in certain relations to other terms but which are not sufficient by themselves for the construction of it.

It is interesting to note that Kant, who believed that the mathematical method of inquiry must prove disastrous in philosophy, nevertheless also believed that the presentation of a philosophical theory in mathematical form could be useful and sometimes even desirable. In a letter to Marcus Herz (end of 1773) in which he tells his friend and former pupil of the good progress of the critical philosophy, he expresses the hope of

1. *Pu. R.* 161, *B* 223.

putting philosophy on a new and permanent foundation and of giving it a form which can 'attract the inflexible mathematician to consider it capable and worthy of his treatment'. After the publication of the *Critique of Pure Reason* he occasionally makes similar remarks in his letters (e.g. letter to Schultz of August 1783).

Kant distinguishes 'three modi of time', namely 'permanence, succession, and simultaneity', and he believes that 'therefore three rules of all temporal relations of appearances, in accordance with which the unity of every appearance is determined with respect to the unity of time, will [logically] precede all objective experience and indeed make it possible'.[1] They are the principles (1) of permanence in substance, (2) of succession, in accordance with the law of causality, in time, and (3) of interaction.

The first analogy or principle of the permanence of substance is formulated as follows: 'In all change of appearances the substance remains, and its quantum in nature neither increases nor decreases.'[2] Kant gives a second formulation of the analogy: 'All change (succession) of appearances is only alteration (of substance).'[3]

Time, which is the form of all empirical perceptions, is itself unchangeable and in any empirical perception is given indirectly by observing change, an observation which, Kant assumes, is possible only through comparing the changing and the abiding elements in the perceptual manifold. Without a permanent feature in perception, there could be no duration and consequently no temporal relation. Kant infers from these premisses that in all objective experience there must be one or more absolutely permanent elements, i.e. a substance or substances.

The inference does not seem valid. From the description of the experience of time through change and the assumption that time is a form of experience it follows only that our experience must contain elements which are relatively permanent. In other

1. *Pu. R.* 159, *B* 219.   2. *Pu. R.* 162, *B* 225.
3. *Pu. R.* 167, *B* 233.

words, while the assumption that there is an absolutely permanent substance does account for our experience of time, it is not the only account possible and not even the only account which is compatible with the teaching of the Transcendental Aesthetic.

It is not surprising that Kant considered the first analogy as formulating a necessary condition of all objective and, therefore, of all scientific experience. In the scientific theories of his day it was never questioned. The analogy, as it stands, only tells us that there must be a permanent substance, not what it is; and it does not commit Kant to the particular conceptions of substance or matter held, e.g., by Newton or Lavoisier. Later conceptions of energy would also have conformed to the principle. Indeed it might seem possible to argue that all that Kant's first analogy really required was that a physical theory should contain some conservation law be it of matter, energy, matter-or-energy or what you will. However, from Kant's discussion of the analogy in the *Critique of Pure Reason* and from his definition of matter in the *Metaphysical Foundations of Natural Science* it seems clear that he conceived the scientific notion of substance as matter. In the latter work matter is defined as 'the mobile in so far as it fills a space, has moving power and can become an object of experience'.[1]

The second analogy, the principle of temporal succession in accordance with the law of causality, is formulated as follows: 'All alterations occur in accordance with the law of the connexion of cause and effect.'[2] It presupposes the first analogy according to which all change (succession of appearances in time) is alteration of substance. Kant, of course, believes himself to have demonstrated already that the applicability of the schematized Category of causality is a necessary condition of objective experience. But, as in the case of the other principles, he considers that the importance of the analogy warrants further demonstrations which will confirm the previous result and throw new light on its function and its place in the system of his philosophy.

1. IV, 480, 496, 534, 554.   2. *Pu. R.* 166, *B* 232.

Just as the first analogy enables us to interpret our experience of change in terms of objective judgements, as opposed to its mere description by subjective or 'as-it-seems-to-me' judgements, so the second analogy provides an objective interpretation of our experience of reversible and irreversible temporal sequences, and of their difference. As an example of a reversible sequence Kant mentions the sequence of perceptions which we have when looking at a house-front piece by piece, beginning at the top and ending at the bottom. The sequence of our perceptions here can be reversed at will by our looking at the same house from bottom to top. As an example of an irreversible sequence he mentions the sequence of perceptions which we have when looking at a ship moving down the river.

If we judge that the sequence of one perception of type A and another perception of type B is irreversible and objective – or as Kant puts it 'in the object' – then we do imply that 'the apprehension of one perception (which occurs) succeeds that of the other (which preceded) *according to a rule*'.[1] 'This rule, however,' says Kant, 'of determining something according to the sequence of time is: that in that which precedes there is to be found the condition according to which the occurrence always (i.e. necessarily) follows. This is why the principle of sufficient reason is the ground of possible objective experience, namely of the objective knowledge of appearances with respect to their relationship in the sequence of time.'[2]

Kant did *not* regard the second analogy as an inductive generalization. He did *not* argue that since all events have had causes in the past all future events will also have causes. He did in particular *not* wish to justify inductive reasoning by an induction which would itself stand in need of the very same kind of justification as it is supposed to provide. What he did want to demonstrate was that we must adopt the regulative principle (pure existence theorem) to the effect that whatever occurrence we consider, 'there is to be found in that which precedes the occurrence, the condition according to which it always follows'. More precisely, he wanted to prove that we

1. *Pu. R.* 170, *B* 238.   2. *Pu. R.* 174, *B* 246.

must adopt this principle *if* we are to be able to make *objective* perceptual judgements about the sequence of appearances in time.

The second analogy does not guarantee the truth of any single objective judgement about the sequence of occurrences, but only its objectivity. It does not replace the search for causal connexion but states a necessary condition for the possibility of any causal inquiry, especially any scientific causal inquiry.

How far has this argumentation been affected by modern advances in physics? Kant has, I believe, demonstrated that the second analogy makes objective perceptual judgements about the sequence of appearances possible. He has, however, not shown that it is the only means of doing so. To see this we only need to note his assumption that an objective sequence of appearances is the same for every observer, and consequently that appearances which are simultaneous for one observer are also simultaneous for every other observer. In modern relativity-physics this assumption has been dropped. This physical theory does not presuppose the second analogy although it does contain *objective* perceptual judgements. In it the second analogy is meaningless or, at least, ambiguous.

Still further, the notion of time which is used in modern physics is incompatible not only with the second analogy (and the third) but also with the Transcendental Aesthetic. The metaphysical presuppositions of Newton are not always also those of relativity-physics, and in so far as the *Critique of Pure Reason* shares the former presuppositions it stands in need of a thorough-going reconstruction. Its doctrine of space and time as *a priori* particulars and forms of perception might need replacing by a new notion of space-time; and its three analogies by a different set. Whitehead's *Concept of Nature* and other works of his could be regarded, I think, as attempts in this direction. Any philosophical physicist undertaking this task could learn a great deal not only from Kant's general approach, but also from the results of his examination of the science of his day.

The third analogy, that of the coexistence according to the law of interaction or community, is formulated as follows: 'All substances in so far as they are perceived as coexistent in space are in thorough-going interaction.'[1] There is no need for us to discuss Kant's new demonstration of the principle. Its task is to show in greater detail than before that provided the first and second analogies are adopted, the adoption of this third one is a necessary and sufficient condition of the possibility of objective empirical judgements about coexisting appearances.

It is clear from what has just been said about the second analogy, particularly with respect to the notion of simultaneity in contemporary physics, that while the principle in conjunction with the first two analogies is a sufficient condition, it is not also a necessary condition of objective experience. It should be obvious that the third analogy is not an empirical generalization or a substitute for any empirical statement or inquiry but merely a regulative principle.

Kant's attempt to prove the analogies, especially the principle of universal causation, is of considerable philosophical interest and is still widely discussed by philosophers and scientists interested in the philosophy of science. It leads to the general question whether propositions such as the analogies can be proved at all; and, if so, what requirements such a proof or disproof would have to fulfil. It is clear that it would have to be quite different from either a logico-mathematical or an experimental one. Thus if we *observed* a swimming cat we should be committed to rejecting the universal empirical proposition that cats cannot swim. It is not conceivable that we should observe an uncaused event by reference to which the universal law of causation could be disproved. We *observe* neither caused nor uncaused events but only events which we either are or are not able to locate in causal chains.

The phrase 'proving the law of universal causation' is in fact highly ambiguous. It may mean showing that a certain body of scientific and commonsense beliefs involves the law as a fundamental assumption. If so, then Kant's proof of the second analogy, considered only in relation to Newtonian

1. *Pu. R.* 180, *B* 256.

science and the commonsense beliefs which are based on it, can certainly not be rejected out of hand. Indeed, the result of the proof is generally accepted. If, however, Kant's proof of the law of universal causation is intended – as he intended it – to show that every theory about what is the case implies this law, then the proof must be invalid for the simple reason that some modern physical theories are incompatible with the law.[1]

There is still at least one other important sense in which the law of universal causation, and consequently any attempt to 'prove' or 'disprove' it, can be controversial. The controversy may turn on the question whether scientific theories in which the law is assumed are likely to be more powerful, say as instruments for prediction, than theories in which it is not assumed. There is no *a priori* answer to this. The decision must in the end depend on the actual development of causal and of non-causal theories. It would seem that at present, and very likely in the near future, the balance is unfavourable to theories embodying the law of universal causation.[2]

Kant's 'axioms of perception' ascribe *a priori* a perceptual feature, namely extension, to all perceptions whether pure or empirical. His 'anticipations of empirical perception' are, so to speak, less informative inasmuch as they ascribe a perceptual feature, intensity, to empirical perceptions only. The 'analogies of experience' do not describe perceptual features at all, but state mere relationships between given perceptions and otherwise unspecified terms. The last of the principles of the pure understanding, the '*postulates of empirical thought in general*', to which we now come and which correspond, it will be remembered, to the Categories of modality, do not contain any information about the world of fact but only about its relation to our cognitive faculties.

The postulates of empirical thought in general are given in Kant's words as follows: ' 1. That which agrees with the formal conditions of experience (with respect to perception and con-

1. See, e.g., Max Born, 'Natural Philosophy of Cause and Chance', Oxford, 1948.
2. See Born *loc. cit.*

cepts) is *possible*. 2. That which is connected with the material conditions of objective experience (of sensation) is *real*. 3. That the connexion of which with the real is determined according to general conditions of objective experience, is (exists as) *necessary*.'[1]

The possibility to which the first postulate refers is not logical possibility but possible existence in an objective experience which is subject to the forms of perception, the axioms of perception, the anticipations of empirical perception, and the analogies of objective experience. For example a Leibnizian monad, as a substance which does not stand in causal relations or relations of interaction with other substances, is logically possible because the concept of it is internally consistent. It is, however, not physically or experientially or, to use a convenient current term, causally possible because it is, to say the least, incompatible with the second and third analogies. Since Leibnizian monads are defined as spiritual substances without location in an absolute space and time they are also incompatible with the formal conditions of perception.

The notion of reality which occurs in the second postulate represents one of the many meanings of an over-worked term. Not only that which is immediately sensed is real: but also that 'which is connected with an empirical perception [and therefore a sensation] in accordance with the analogies of objective experience . . .'[2] This second postulate constitutes a definition of scientific reality. In order to be adequate to later scientific development Kant's reference to 'the' analogies of objective experience would have to be broadened to admit other kinds of analogy as well.

In the third postulate the notion of necessity is again not the logical notion. The general conditions of objective experience include not only its *a priori* conditions but also the empirical laws of nature. What follows from them is causally but not logically necessary. That all men must die is causally necessary because deducible from the empirical laws of nature; but it is not logically necessary, since the negation of it, the statement

1. *Pu. R.* 185, 186, *B* 265, 266.   2. *Pu. R.* 189, *B* 272.

that there exists an immortal man – although false – is not self-contradictory.

4. The Phenomenal and the Noumenal World

The Transcendental Aesthetic and the Transcendental Analytic are Kant's account of the structure of objective experience. As it stands, this account certainly implies the existence of an unknown and unknowable X which 'affects' our senses with something which is 'transformed' into objective and scientific reality by being 'subjected' to certain forms – on the one hand to the forms of perception, and on the other to the form of the understanding, the latter being simply the sum total of synthetic *a priori* principles.

The conclusion of the Transcendental Aesthetic that the two forms of perception, space and time, are empirically real, but transcendentally ideal, might be modified without completely relinquishing the assumptions on which it is based. It is indeed just possible to argue that all that follows from them is the doctrine that there *may be* things in themselves which are not located in space or time. One might even compare the possibility of things in themselves existing and being different from things for us with a suggestion which Kant makes – the possibility that sense and understanding 'perhaps spring from a common, but to us unknown root'.[1] He has left the latter possibility alone, one might say, because it would be fruitless to inquire into the unknown and unknowable. Perhaps he would have been well advised to deal with the former possibility in the same way.

At the end of the Transcendental Analytic even the most insensitive and self-willed reader must, it would seem to me, feel convinced that the thing in itself is an important part of the Kantian philosophy. This conviction will grow stronger with every further step into the system. It is the fundamental assumption of the Analytic that the synthetic unity of a mani-

1. *Pu. R.* 46, *B* 29.

fold of perception is *conferred upon it* by the pure (as opposed to the empirical or introspective) self-consciousness of the subject. Without the synthetic unity so conferred upon the manifold there could be no object of experience. In other words, Kant holds that since there are objects of experience, there must be things in themselves; and that since we apprehend objects of experience we cannot possibly apprehend things in themselves.

The doctrine that the objects of experience are not things in themselves and that things in themselves are unknowable is an important corollary of the inquiry whose aim it was to establish which of the principles of objective experience are synthetic *a priori* and to account for their synthetic *a priori* character. Kant calls it 'transcendental' idealism because the inquiry which led to it had also been called 'transcendental'.

Transcendental idealism is not concerned with relationships between the objects of experience and perception. It is in particular not concerned with the relation between empirical or introspective self-awareness and 'the existence of objects in space outside myself'.[1] As regards *this* relation Kant distinguishes the view of 'material' or empirical idealism, that introspective self-awareness 'is the only immediate experience and that from it the existence of external things is only inferred ...',[2] from his own view of empirical realism, which holds that 'the experience of outer objects is truly immediate and that only by means of it ... inner experience is possible.'[3]

Empirical or material idealism is according to Kant either problematic or dogmatic, the former if it considers the existence of objects in space outside us as dubious and undemonstrable; the latter if it considers the assumption of their existence false and logically impossible. It may be doubted whether he was right in regarding Descartes as a problematic idealist. If he did, as Kant says, consider 'only *one* empirical assertion, namely *I am*, as an indubitable starting point', he still believed himself to have demonstrated the existence of external objects as an indubitable conclusion in the course of his inquiry. It is

1. *Pu. R.* 191, *B* 275. 2. *Pu. R. loc. cit.*
3. *Pu. R.* 192, *B* 276.

possible, however, that Kant like many others may have believed that Descartes' argument was fallacious and that therefore his conclusion was no solution of the problem.

It may equally be doubted whether Kant was right in regarding Berkeley as a dogmatic idealist. Berkeley did not consider the assumption of external objects to be false. He only regarded its analysis by the realists as inadequate. He did not, however, make his position as unambiguously clear as it now seems to most of his (non-Marxist) commentators to have been. Yet even if we were determined to regard Berkeley as a forerunner of modern phenomenalism his theory is incompatible with Kant's transcendentally idealist and empirically realist view of the external world.

Kant's demonstration of his own 'empirical realism' is brief but rather complicated. It is based on an examination of empirical situations involving introspective self-consciousness. His main point is that in any such situation 'I am conscious of my existence as being determined in time'[1], and consequently am conscious of change and of something permanent. This permanent feature, however, 'cannot be anything in me', because 'my existence can in the first instance only be determined by it. Therefore, its perception is possible only through a thing outside myself...'[2]

That 'the consciousness of my own existence is at the same time an immediate consciousness of the existence of other things outside me' is for Kant an empirical fact.[3] If we are to accept this then the view that we *infer* the existence of external objects cannot be true, for the very simple reason that we do not make any inference at all. What, if I am not mistaken, makes Kant's refutation of empirical idealism difficult to understand, is that it appears to prove what should be self-evident. In this connexion it is worth noting that the refutation of idealism had been quite differently formulated in the first edition of the *Critique of Pure Reason*.

The objects of experience are the only objects which we can know, i.e. perceive and judge to be instances of the Categories;

1. *Pu. R.* 191, *B* 275.   2. *Pu. R. loc. cit.*   3. *Pu. R. loc. cit.*

and the Categories cannot be applied to anything outside possible objective experience. Yet we are committed, according to
Kant, to the thesis *that* there are things in themselves although
we cannot know what they are. Indeed, as has been pointed
out by Schopenhauer, we cannot even properly speak of things
in themselves or the thing in itself, since in doing so we seem
to apply the Category of plurality or of unity to that which
ex hypothesi cannot come under any Category.

Kant calls the things in themselves '*noumena*' because they
are entities of the understanding to which no objects of experience can ever correspond, and contrasts them with '*phenomena*'
which are or can be objects of experience. The conception of a
noumenon is self-consistent and formed in an entirely straightforward manner by means of the rules which govern negation
of concepts. If we know the rules which govern a concept, say
'coloured', and the rules governing the auxiliary term 'not',
then we know *ipso facto* the rules which govern the negation of
the concept, namely, 'not-coloured'. It is, in particular, not
necessary to the negation of the concept that we should know
instances of it, even if the concept itself cannot be formed without knowledge of instances.

Similarly if we have formed the concept of an object of
experience or *phenomenon* – which is exactly what we have done
in following the argument of the Aesthetic and the Analytic –
and if we know the rules governing the auxiliary term 'not',
then we have *ipso facto* formed the concept of a *not-phenomenon*
or '*noumenon*'. The difference between 'not-coloured' on the
one hand, and 'not-*phenomenon*' ('*noumenon*') on the other, lies
mainly in that while we may, and in fact do, experience not-
coloured entities, e.g. pains, *noumena* are defined as something
which we cannot experience. The concept of a *noumenon* is, as
Kant puts it, a limiting concept.

'If by *noumenon* we understand a thing *in so far as it is not an
object of our sense-perception* ... then it is a *noumenon* in the negative sense of the term.'[1] In this sense the concept of a *noumenon*
carries no metaphysical commitments with it further than the

1. *Pu. R.* 209, *B* 307.

concept of a phenomenon. If, for example, *phenomena* are the subject matter of ,natural science then this just means that *noumena* (*non-phenomena*) are not the subject matter of natural science.

It is, as Kant points out, very easy to replace the negative concept of a *noumenon*, surreptitiously and illegitimately, by a positive one. 'If we understand [by a *noumenon*] an object of *a perception which is not sense-perception*, then we assume a special kind of perception, namely intellectual perception, which is not our kind ... and this would be the *noumenon* in the positive sense of the term.'[1]

A defect in Kant's distinction between the negative and the positive conception of a *noumenon* is its insufficient generality. The concept of a *noumenon* is positive if its use, besides being governed by the rules governing '*phenomenon*' and 'not', is also governed by other rules. If for example we conceive, with Kant, a *noumenon* or thing in itself as being not only a non-phenomenon but something which somehow affects our senses, then our concept is no longer merely negative. Kant's assertion that in the *Critique of Pure Reason* he uses the concept of a *noumenon* only as a negative and limiting concept is thus incompatible with his actual use. It is, I believe, possible to reconstruct the *Critique* in such a way that the concept of a *noumenon* is in fact used only as a negative concept. But it would be a mistake to regard such reconstruction as a mere interpretation of Kant's philosophy.

On Kant's part the distinction between the empirical reality and the transcendental ideality of objective experience does not hide any attempt to interfere with scientific inquiry, or deduce empirical laws from *a priori* premisses. Such attempts became possible to his self-appointed successors only after radical changes in the fundamental assumptions of the critical philosophy. To the proper work of the scientist the distinction was, as Kant insisted, irrelevant.

It is, however, of great importance to the critical philosophy as a whole, since this philosophy tries to understand our ex-

1. *Pu. R. loc. cit.*

perience not only of fact but also of moral obligation and of aesthetic and religious values. Kant believes that without distinguishing between transcendental and empirical reality the apparent conflict between science on the one hand and morality and religion on the other cannot be resolved. By showing that *noumena* cannot be known but can be thought without contradiction, Kant believes he has shown the possibility of *faith* in moral freedom, the immortality of the soul and the existence of God. 'I had', he says,[1] 'to abolish *knowledge* in order to make room for faith.'

5. Kant and Rationalism

It has always been an ambition of philosophers to prove that entities which appear different are really similar or to prove that entities which appear to be similar are really different. In Kant's day the former ambition was the one in the ascendant. Thus the empiricists tried to show that all concepts are abstracted from perceived particulars, while the rationalists tried to show that no concepts are so derived because, contrary to all appearance, there are no perceived particulars. 'Leibniz *intellectualized* appearances, just as Locke ... sensualized the concepts of the understanding ...'[2]

So far Kant had mainly been concerned with establishing that we do, and legitimately, employ *a priori* concepts and synthetic *a priori* principles. His argument is thus more obviously incompatible with the empiricist thesis than with that of the rationalists. This may be one reason why the last pages of the Transcendental Analytic are devoted to a repudiation of rationalism in the shape of an express refutation of Leibniz's philosophy and to a diagnosis of the source of its errors. Another reason may perhaps be found in the fact that the philosophy of Leibniz had taken deeper roots in the Germany of Kant's day than any other philosophy. Kant himself actually used textbooks produced by Leibnizians, in his lectures.

Yet another reason may have been his fear lest some of his

1. *Pu. R.* 19, *B* xxx.   2. *Pu. R.* 221, *B* 327.

readers, the less acute or the too clever among them, should be tempted to interpret the critical philosophy as being a mere variant of Berkeleian empiricism or of the Leibnizian rational-ism. At any rate the fear was justified. There were those who could not distinguish between the critical philosophy and Berkeley's idealism; and, to Kant's greater chagrin, also those who considered his position as being in essence that of Leibniz. Indeed he thought it necessary to write a monograph (over sixty pages in the *Akademie* edition of his works) against Herr Eberhard who believed that Kant had been fully anticipated by Leibniz.[1]

Kant's criticism of Leibniz is no less relevant to contempor-ary controversies than his criticism of Locke and Hume has proved to be. Attempts to analyse away perceived particulars are to be found, for example, in the idealist theory of truth as coherence and even in some logical positivists such as Neurath. These attempts are probably symptomatic of a perennial philo-sophic tendency. It is perhaps unlikely that the thesis that judgements about perceived particulars 'really' assert rela-tions between concepts will ever lose its attraction, which seems to be based on some obscure desire that reality should be fully rational.

Kant believes that the whole system of Leibniz stems from the elementary fallacy of thinking that by denying the antece-dent in a hypothetical statement, you have denied the conse-quent. From an implication 'if it is Sunday then the shops are closed' one cannot reason that if today happens not to be Sunday then the shops will not be closed. Kant alleges that Leibniz has committed this fallacy. The proposition: 'What-ever universally belongs to a concept or contradicts one, be-longs also to, or contradicts, every particular instance falling under it' is true. But Leibniz has falsely inferred from it that 'what does *not* universally belong to a concept does *not* belong to every particular instance falling under it'.[2]

1. See Kant's *On an alleged discovery showing all the recent criticism of pure reason to have been superfluous* (1790), VIII, 185 ff.

2. *Pu. R.* 226, *B* 337.

D

The second proposition is false on Kantian principles since the attribute of being at a certain place or at a certain time does not belong to a concept but belongs to its instances. For example 'being in his kennel at six o'clock today' does not belong to the concept 'dog'; but this does not hinder Pluto, who is an instance of 'dog', from being there at that time. (It is only fair to add that Leibniz's answer to Kant's accusation would consist in pointing out that on his view temporal and spatial characteristics are relational and that a statement which ascribes an absolute spatial or temporal location to Pluto, though practically convenient, is philosophically objectionable.)

Kant's point can be put in another way by distinguishing, with him, between *sensibilia* and *intelligibilia*. A *sensibile* or a sensible instance of a concept is an instance which has spatial or temporal location or both (in absolute space or time). An *intelligibile* or intelligible instance is an instance (of a concept) which has no such location. According to Kant, Pluto the dog, and all objects of experience, are *sensibilia*, while things in themselves or *noumena* are *intelligibilia*. According to Leibniz, there are only *intelligibilia*, some of which, like Pluto, may *appear* to be *sensibilia*.

Kant points out that Leibniz's famous principle of the identity of indiscernibles is a direct consequence of his doctrine that there are no *sensibilia*, a doctrine which, so Kant believes, is due to the above-mentioned fallacy. It is indeed logically impossible that two different *intelligibilia* should fall under the same concepts since they would be absolutely indiscernible and thus really only one *intelligibile*. For example the *intelligibile* called the 'first prime number' is absolutely (or numerically) identical with the *intelligibile* called 'the number 2'. On the other hand two *sensibilia*, say Pluto and Fido, would, even if they fell under the same concepts, be numerically different: they would be two dogs. If the doctrine of the Transcendental Aesthetic is true, then the principle of the identity of indiscernibles must be false. (But Leibniz would, of course, not accept that doctrine.) In other words, if the doctrine of the Transcendental Aesthetic is true, then Leibniz has not seen that the instances of the *same* concept may yet be different. He has fallen a victim to the ambiguity (or 'amphiboly') of the comparative notions of sameness and difference.

Kant accuses Leibniz of another mistake. He overlooked the ambiguity of the concepts of compatibility and incompatibility, whose meaning is different according as they are applied to concepts or to their sensible instances. Attributed to this same mistake is Leibniz's optimism, more especially his doctrine that evil is a mere negation and, therefore, is unreal. Reality for Leibniz is fully describable in terms of affirmative concepts, i.e. without making use of the rules governing negation. A system of affirmative concepts cannot contain any mutually incompatible concepts. In the order of the world Leibniz regards the existence of evil as an apparent incompatibility. Since, however – and here, for Kant, lies the fallacy – the concepts which describe reality cannot be mutually incompatible, their (intelligible) instances, which are reality, cannot be mutually incompatible, so evil cannot be real. Leibniz's confusion here is, I believe, easily seen even without the assistance of the critical philosophy. Yet Kant's discussion of it does point to a deeper reason from which the confusion follows – the assimilation of perception to judgement.

Kant tries to show that Leibniz's monadology and the relational character of space and time also follow from the thesis that all instances of concepts are *intelligibilia*. It may, however, well be that Leibniz's doctrines of space and time and of the monads (which are non-material substances) are for him more fundamental. The monadology is nowadays of hardly more than historical interest, while to discuss the issue of space and time as between Kant and Newton on the one hand and Leibniz on the other would take us far beyond the scope of the present book.[1]

1. For an illuminating discussion of the question see: C. D. Broad, *Leibniz's last controversy with the Newtonians* in *Selected Essays, vol. I.*

6. Categories and *A Priori* Principles in Contemporary Philosophy

It is impossible to trace here the influence of the Transcendental Analytic on contemporary philosophy or even on contemporary English philosophy. It is nevertheless worth while to show that Kant's theory of *a priori* concepts and principles has had its effect on some contemporary English philosophers. None of those whom I have chosen as examples is a Kantian either in the proper sense of the term or in the loose sense which has for a long time been current in the English-speaking countries. To be a Kantian is not to interpret Kant in the manner of Coleridge; and it is not to interpret him in the manner of the English Hegelians who valued Kant as merely the forerunner of Hegel. The philosophers whom I am here ruling out are numerous. But the influence of a great thinker is not properly measured by the number of those who profess to be his disciples or who loudly praise his insights. It is better seen in the number of his distinctive doctrines which have come to be so generally accepted that his name is no longer attached to them.

I have already discussed the importance of the Transcendental Analytic for the subsequent philosophy of science. It exemplifies a general method for making explicit the principles which, while neither empirical generalizations nor analytic elucidations of the meaning of terms, are yet necessary conditions of the objective character of the objective empirical judgements belonging to a body of scientific theory. I have also argued that Kant was mistaken in regarding Newton's physics as containing all the possible types of objective empirical judgement and consequently in regarding his own list of *a priori* principles as complete.

Kant sees the difference between merely subjective perceptual judgements and objective empirical judgements in the fact that the latter involve, as the former do not, the application of Categories. It is, therefore, not possible so to *analyse* any objec-

tive empirical judgement as to obtain its equivalent in perceptual judgements (or in any combination of them according to
the rules which govern the auxiliary terms 'not', 'or', and 'if-
then'). That such an analysis is possible, and that consequently
we do not use *a priori* concepts, was the position of Berkeley
and his followers in the eighteenth century, of Mach and
Avenarius in the nineteenth, and of the English phenomenalists
in the twentieth.

The careful work done by the last-mentioned philosophers
in their attempts to analyse objective empirical propositions in
terms of perceptual propositions or, in more recent terminology, to analyse physical-object statements in terms of sense-
data propositions, has been particularly instructive. In them
the powerful, ingenious apparatus of modern deductive logic
has been used. These attempts are now generally regarded as
having failed, a failure which goes to support a fundamental
doctrine of the Transcendental Analytic, namely that all objective empirical propositions involve the application of Categories, i.e. of applicable but not abstracted concepts.

This view has been expressed, for example, by C. D. Broad:
'The notion of Physical Object cannot have been abstracted
from the data of sense. It is a Category, and is defined by
Postulates.' This is quite clearly a Kantian statement, especially
since 'Postulates', whatever else they may be, are certainly not
analytic propositions or empirical generalizations.[1]

A. J. Ayer, who shows greater sympathy with the pheno-
menalist position, comes to the conclusion that it may be best
'to treat our beliefs about physical objects as constituting a
theory, the function of which is to explain the course of our
sensory experiences. The statements which are expressed in
terms of the theory may not then be capable of being repro-
duced exactly as statements about sense-data ... Nevertheless
they will function only as a means of grouping sense-data ...
It may then be required of the philosopher to make clear in
what this organization consists ... Thus, to echo Kant, he may
be represented as trying to answer the question, How is the

1. *The Mind and its Place in Nature*, 1923, p. 220.

physical object language possible?'[1] Kant's *a priori* principles
function indeed as 'a means of grouping sense-data', i.e. they
confer synthetic unity and thus objectivity on a manifold of
perception.

Kant's objection to empiricism is repeated in Bertrand Russell's *Human Knowledge* (1948) and takes up most of the last
chapter of the book. This is perhaps surprising in a philosopher
whose respect for Kant's powerful mind appears to be matched
by an almost equally strong dislike for his philosophical system, a dislike frequently, and at times forcefully, expressed.
Russell comes to the conclusion that the empiricist doctrine
'that all our synthetic knowledge is based on experience ...' is
either false or unknowable.[2] He argues that 'the inferences
from facts to other facts can only be valid if the world has certain characteristics which are not logically necessary. Are these
characteristics known to us by experience? It would seem not.'[3]

Russell must thus hold that in our thinking about matters of fact we have to assume principles, 'postulates of scientific inference' as he calls them, neither logically necessary
(analytic), nor empirical (*a posteriori*). 'They are known in the
sense that we generalize *in accordance* with them when we use
experience to persuade us of a universal proposition such as
"Dogs bark".'[4] Russell thus believes that objective experience
presupposes non-analytic and non-*a-posteriori* principles, in
other words that 'we are in possession of' synthetic *a priori*
principles.[5]

But unlike Kant, Russell sees no need for a Transcendental
Deduction of these principles. All he offers is but what Kant
found in 'the famous Locke', namely an '*empirical deduction*
which shows the manner in which a concept (and a principle)
has been acquired by experience and reflection about it, but
which consequently does not concern the rightfulness of the
possession, but only the mere fact from which it has arisen'.[6]
What Russell tells us in effect is no more than that 'the forming

1. *Aristotelian Society Proceedings*, vol. 47, p. 196.
2. *Op. cit.* p. 525.   3. *Loc. cit.*   4. *Op. cit.* p. 526, my italics.
5. *Pu. R.* 28, *B* 3.   6. *Pu. R.* 100, *B* 117.

of inferential habits which lead to true expectations is part of the adaptation to the environment upon which biological survival depends'. He offers a scientific statement instead of a more detailed account of the logical nature of his postulates of scientific inference.

Kant, I have argued,[1] in spite of his explicit definitions, conceives his synthetic *a priori* principles as *judgements* (1) the negations of which are not self-contradictory and (2) which are logically independent of judgements describing sense-impressions. He also believed that they do not admit of any alternatives, and indeed he had never any occasion to consider the kind of conflict which exists between two different systems of synthetic *a priori* principles; for example, between those on the one hand which express necessary conditions of the objective character of the judgements of relativity-physics, and on the other his own, which perform a similar function for the physics of Newton.

If two judgements are mutually incompatible then one or both of them must be false. Yet conflicting *a priori* principles cannot be said to be false; at least, not in the sense in which empirical or logical propositions are. To account for the conflict between such principles one must either give a satisfactory new definition of 'truth' and 'falsehood' which would have to differ from the corresponding definitions of the notions of empirical and of logical truth and falsehood; or else one would have to drop the assumption that the principles are judgements at all.

The latter course seems to me the more promising, and I have argued elsewhere[2] that metaphysical propositions of the type to which Kant's *a priori* principles belong should be interpreted as rules which are conformed to in the construction of theories of a certain type. Thus, for example, the Kantian principles can be regarded as rules governing the Kantian Categories which are conformed to in the construction of mechanistic theories of the sort to which Newtonian physics

1. § 3 of chapter 1.
2. *Conceptual Thinking* (New York, 1959) pp. 264 ff.

belongs. Rules are propositions in a wider sense of 'proposition', a sense in which we should require, e.g., the possibility of entailment and of incompatibility between propositions but not also that they should be – either logically or empirically – true or false.

While there is, so I believe, no doubt that Kant conceived his synthetic *a priori* principles to be true judgements, he yet frequently speaks of them expressly as rules. Thus the pure understanding, which is the source of the synthetic *a priori* principles, is called a 'faculty of rules'.[1] The synthetic *a priori* principles are regarded 'as nothing else but rules for the objective use of the Categories'.[2] Moreover, the analogies of objective experience and the postulates of empirical thought in general are called 'regulative' in a more specific sense.[3] On the other hand Kant also seems to think that the synthetic *a priori* principles are judgements *about* the 'possibility of objective experience' in very much the same sense in which *a posteriori* judgements are *about* what is given in perception. In fact he does not distinguish at all clearly between rules and other types of proposition.

1. E.g., *Pu. R.* 146, *B* 197.   2. *Pu. R.* 147, *B* 200.
3. *Pu. R.* 161, *B* 222.

CHAPTER FIVE

THE ILLUSIONS OF METAPHYSICS

1. The Source of the Ideas of Pure Reason and of Absolute Metaphysical Judgements

WE can say of the *a priori* principles which Kant has now shown to be necessary conditions for the objective character of a type – not, as I have argued, of every type – of objective empirical judgement, that they are genuine metaphysical propositions. They are valid in that they are presuppositions of Newtonian science and of 'commonsense' objective experience. The term 'presupposition' is a vague one, and has been greatly misused; but its use in referring to Kant's position should be harmless, once the main theses of the Analytic have been understood.

Metaphysical presuppositions, whether of science, of mathematics, or of any other theory, must be distinguished from absolute metaphysical propositions. The latter are not necessary conditions of the objective character of a non-metaphysical theory, but apparently constitute the body of an autonomous science. They are not *about the possibility* of objective experience, but apparently about some peculiar subject matter of their own.

The task of Kant's Transcendental Dialectic is (1) to show that belief in such absolute metaphysical principles arises from the very nature of our thinking about matters of fact; (2) to give a complete list of these principles and of the *a priori* notions which are involved in them; (3) to demonstrate that their claim to give us knowledge of matters of fact is illegitimate; and lastly (4) to explain their proper and legitimate function in our theoretical endeavour. The strategy is analogous to that of the Analytic. To the method used in the Analytic for discovering the Categories, there corresponds here in the Dialectic a method for discovering the Ideas of Reason, i.e. *a priori* notions which are neither abstracted from nor applicable to experience. To the transition in the Analytic from the allegedly complete list of Categories to the synthetic *a priori* Principles of the pure Understanding there corresponds in the Dialectic the transition from the Ideas to the *a priori* Principles of Reason, i.e. the absolute metaphysical principles.

There is, however, no Transcendental Deduction of the Ideas. Instead Kant shows that their application to (alleged) matters of fact is unjustified. In other words to the Transcendental Deduction of the Categories there corresponds in the Dialectic the proof that there can be no such deduction of the Ideas. This proof – or disproof – Kant regards as highly important. Absolute metaphysics (the term is not Kant's own, but conveys his meaning) is no ordinary illusion which can be removed with sufficient logical care. It can be recognized as illusion but it is irremovable. 'The transcendental illusion . . . does not vanish even when it has been detected and when its illusory character stands clearly revealed by transcendental criticism (for instance, the illusion in the proposition: The world must have a beginning in time).'[1]

Kant's claim to have found a clue for listing all the Ideas of Reason and consequently all absolute metaphysical principles is again based on his confidence in the completeness of the traditional logic – its completeness this time in listing all the possible forms not of judgement but of mediate inference. He holds that just as the Categories are embodied in the judgement-forms, so the Ideas are embodied in the forms of inference. For us it is again important to distinguish between his large claim to have discovered all possible Ideas and absolute metaphysical principles, and the more moderate claim, implied in the other, that he has discovered at least some of them. It would indeed be foolish to let the neatly, for some tastes too neatly, systematic presentation of the Transcendental Dialectic blind us to the importance of the thoughts which it conveys. They are hardly

1. *Pu. R.* 237, *B* 353.

less relevant to contemporary philosophical issues than are the thoughts contained in the equally neat and rigid system of the Transcendental Analytic.

Kant calls the power of mediate inference 'reason' in a narrow sense of the term in which it is distinguished from understanding, which is the power of making objective perceptual judgements by the application of the Categories. Since syllogistic inference is for him the only mediate inference, 'reason' can also be said to be the power of syllogistic inference. The only type of inference other than this which Kant recognizes, is that called 'immediate'; in which the conclusion follows directly from one premiss as, e.g., 'Some men are mortal' or 'No men are immortal' follows from 'All men are mortal'. Immediate inference is always assigned to the understanding.

In a mediate or syllogistic inference, e.g. from 'All men are mortal' and 'All scholars are men' to the conclusion 'Therefore all scholars are mortal' there must always be two premisses. The premiss which contains the predicate of the conclusion, 'mortal' in our example, is called the major. The one which contains the subject of the conclusion, in our example 'scholar', is called the minor. Kant distinguishes between three kinds of mediate, syllogistic inferences, or as he also calls them 'inferences of reason'; namely that in which the major premiss is always a categorical, that in which it is a hypothetical, and that in which it is a disjunctive judgement, i.e. he divides inferences according to the so-called 'relation' of the major premiss.[1]

In a mediate inference we do not make any *new* objective empirical judgement but state the deductive relationship between given judgements. In particular, if a certain judgement is given we look for two others which could serve as premisses from which it follows as their conclusion. Since the premisses themselves are only used in the inference and not proved by it we must, if we want to prove them, look for further premisses from which they can be deduced. In order in this way to

1. See chapter III, § 3.

prove our major premiss 'All men are mortal' we should have
to show it as following from some *more general* proposition,
say 'All animals are mortal' which, if we can add 'All men are
animals', would prove it.

Now 'All animals are mortal' is a *common* major premiss not
only with respect to the conclusion 'All men are mortal', but
also with respect to 'All tigers are mortal', 'All fish are mortal', and so on. It thus connects all these propositions and gives
them a systematic unity which they do not possess if regarded
as separate judgements. Such unity among our judgements
increases with every further such arrangement of them into
syllogistic form and in particular with any further demonstration that the major premiss of a given syllogism is itself a conclusion which follows from more general premisses.

We have been speaking of syllogistic inference and with it
of reason, which is the faculty of such inference; and we can
see two characteristics of it which are of importance for the
understanding of Kant's argument in the Transcendental Dialectic. 'First, the inference of reason is not concerned with
perceptions by bringing them under rules (as is the understanding with its Categories), but with concepts and judgements.'[1] Secondly, in giving systematic unity to judgements
through arranging them in syllogistic order, it tries to find a
more general major premiss for every one of its syllogistically
arranged judgements, and thus the ultimate premiss in every
chain of syllogisms. It tries, in Kant's somewhat obscure words
'to the conditional knowledge of the understanding, to find
the unconditioned', in order to 'bring the former to completion'.[2]

Kant, however, makes his meaning quite clear by a distinction between the logical maxim of syllogistic arrangement and
the fundamental principle of pure reason. The maxim is a piece
of logical advice and could be formulated as follows: If you
want to give systematic unity to your judgements by arranging
them syllogistically, you must find to every condition or premiss a further condition or premiss, and try to proceed in that

1. *Pu. R.* 242, *B* 363.   2. *Pu. R. loc. cit.*

way towards the ultimate condition, which, being itself dependent on no further condition, would be unconditioned or absolute. It is important to note that this useful maxim does not imply that there *is* any ultimate, unconditioned condition. In this respect it reminds us of the moral maxim that we should all try to become saints, a maxim which, however valuable it may be, certainly does not imply that if we set out to follow it we shall or possibly can become saints.

As contrasted with this logical maxim of pure reason its fundamental principle is the assumption that the chain of premisses or conditions actually has a last unconditioned or absolute member and is, therefore, able to be completed and so, in a sense, completely given. The transition from the maxim to the principle is analogous to the transition from the maxim that we should try to become saints, to the assumption that we can. It is equally unwarranted in both cases.

'The logical maxim cannot become a fundamental principle of *pure reason* unless we assume that if the conditioned is given, the whole sequence of subordinate conditions, which consequently is itself unconditioned, is also given ... Whether this principle that the sequence of conditions ... reaches the unconditioned is or is not objectively valid; and what consequences follow from this for the empirical use of reason ... will be our business in the Transcendental Dialectic, which we now intend to develop from its sources which are deeply hidden in human reason.'[1]

The fundamental principle of reason thus assumes as given completely that systematic unity in all the judgements of our understanding, towards which the logical maxim *only bids us to strive*. Claiming in this sense to confer the unity of a perfect logical order on our judgements, it reminds us of the fundamental principle of the Understanding, the unity of pure apperception, which claims to confer synthetic unity on the manifold of perception, as though our judgements furnished Reason with a kind of manifold of its own. But while the subjective claim of the unity of pure apperception was shown to

1. *Pu. R.* 243, 244, *B* 364–6.

be rightful, Kant means to demonstrate that the subjective claim of this so-called fundamental principle of reason is the source of antinomies and other fallacies and, therefore, wholly spurious and unjustified.

Kant's sharp distinction between a maxim saying how the next member in an ascending syllogistic chain is found and the assumption that the links in their totality are given, shows striking similarity to a highly important distinction in the modern theory of sets and the foundations of mathematical analysis. I refer to the distinction between a rule which allows us to construct the next member of an 'infinite' sequence and the assumption that the whole sequence is given in its totality. The need for the distinction lies in the logical antinomies or contradictions implicit in systems where this assumption is made. It is another tribute to Kant's remarkable penetration that many philosophical logicians consider the assumption of infinite yet completely given totalities as illegitimate for reasons very similar to those which he put forward against the fundamental principle of pure reason.

The principle that 'if the conditioned is given, the whole sequence of subordinate conditions ... is also given' leads according to Kant to three sources of fallacy, due to the assumption of three types of completed sequence corresponding to the three possible forms of syllogistic inference. If we ascend along a syllogistic chain from premiss to higher premiss by means of categorical syllogisms, then the fundamental principle of pure reason demands that we arrive at length 'at a subject which is not itself a predicate'. If the ascent takes place by means of hypothetical syllogisms, then the principle demands an ultimate 'presupposition which itself presupposes nothing else'. Lastly if the journey is undertaken by way of disjunctive syllogisms, the principle demands 'an aggregate of the members of the (disjunctive) division, – such as requires no more in order to complete the division of the concept'.[1]

The fundamental principle of reason thus demands three kinds of absolute or unconditioned unity. Kant identifies them

1. *Pu. R.* 252, *B* 379, 380.

with three Transcendental Ideas: '*first* the absolute (unconditioned) unity of the thinking subject, *second* the absolute unity of the sequence of the conditions of the appearance, *third* the absolute unity of the condition of objects of thought in general. The thinking subject is the subject matter of (speculative) *psychology*, the totality of appearances (the world) that of (speculative) *cosmology*, and the entity which contains the highest condition of the possibility of everything which can be thought (the entity of all entities), that of theology.'[1]

The logical maxim of syllogistic order which demands that we should, step by step, proceed from premiss to higher premiss can be followed within the field of the understanding, that is to say, for any, limited or unlimited, set of objective perceptual judgements. The assumption of the completed process cannot be realized in this field and is indeed the source of antinomies. It transcends all possible experience or is, as Kant puts it, transcendent. Consequently no object of experience can possibly correspond to any of the three Ideas.

2. The Illusions of Speculative Psychology

Many philosophers before Kant and some philosophers after him, for example his one-time disciple Fichte, believed in the possibility of a science of the self which can be developed, like pure mathematics or logic, in a purely *a priori* fashion without recourse to any empirical observation or experiment. This putative *a priori* psychology went under the names of 'speculative' or 'rational' psychology. The very thought of such a 'science' seems strange to us who have seen the birth and will, as I believe, continue for a long time to see the perpetuation, of an experimental psychology so obstinately experimental that some of its exponents think proper to frown upon introspection even when introspecting in pursuance of their inquiry. Rational Psychology is a thing of the past. Its fallacies, however, like all the others examined in the Dialectic, have lost

1. *Pu. R.* 258, *B* 391.

none of their vitality, sometimes even being hailed nowadays as new and profound discoveries.

Thus the theme which Heidegger, in what seems to me provocatively Kantian terminology, calls 'the Analytic of Existence (*Dasein*)' is no more than a variation of the old theme of rational psychology. In the first chapter of the first part of his *Sein und Zeit* (the long title of which duly contains the term 'Transcendental') he says that 'the existent, the analysis of which is our task, is we ourselves. The being of this existent is always *mine*. In its being this existent concerns itself with its own being.'[1] There are other examples of rational psychology to be found in contemporary philosophical works, but I should hardly expect to find many presented so precisely in terms which Kant used as key-terms in the *Critique of Pure Reason*.

In the Analytic of Concepts Kant has drawn a sharp distinction between the '*I think* which must be *capable* of accompanying all my presentations',[2] thereby giving them synthetic unity, and the empirical, introspected, self which is itself a presentation. To be truly *a priori* rational psychology must have for its subject the former, i.e. the self of pure self-consciousness. This however is *not*, according to Kant, an object of experience. It is a necessary condition of objective experience and so of the applicability of the Categories. It is not an instance of any Category.

Now rational psychology consists in the 'application' of Categories – in particular the Category of substance – to a pure self which is assumed to be free from any empirical admixture. It does this mainly by means of a fallacious syllogism. The fallacy consists in using the terms 'subject' and 'substance' in two different senses. In the major premiss of the syllogism 'subject' is used in the purely logical sense of 'subject of a categorical judgement'. In the minor premiss it is used in the sense of the *I think* of pure self-consciousness. 'Substance' similarly, is used in the major premiss in the logical sense of 'that which can be the subject but not the predicate of cate-

1. *Op. cit.* p. 41.   2. See ch. III, § 5.

gorical judgements', and in the minor in the sense in which only a (thinkable *and* perceivable) object of experience can be a substance. The *logical* sense of 'subject' and 'substance' will be distinguished by capitals in the sequel, for the sake of clearness.

Kant expresses the fundamental fallacy as follows:[1] (1) 'What cannot be thought except as a SUBJECT also does not exist except as a SUBJECT and is therefore SUBSTANCE'; (2) 'A thinking being considered merely as such cannot be thought except as a subject.' Therefore (3) 'A thinking being only exists ... as substance.' The fallacy is evident; and, as Kant shows by considering the premisses and the conclusion separately,[2] the fallacy can also be seen clearly if we notice that the premisses are analytic judgements which merely elucidate the meanings of SUBJECT, SUBSTANCE, and subject, while the conclusion is synthetic. From analytic premisses a synthetic conclusion cannot be legitimately inferred. If this were possible we could create matters of fact by suitably defining our terms.

If the thesis of rational psychology that the self or soul is a substance is an illusion of absolute metaphysics, then the same must be true of the theses (1) that it is simple substance; (2) that it is a substance which remains numerically identical throughout the passage of time; and (3) that it stands in relation to possible objects in space, in particular to its own body.

3. The Illusions of Speculative Cosmology

If the world or cosmos is conceived as the sum total of all things in space and time, speculative or rational cosmology will be that branch of absolute metaphysics which consists of such synthetic *a priori* propositions as are about 'the world'. Kant shows that this alleged *a priori* science too must lead to fallacies – this time to antinomies which only the critical philosophy can resolve.

By an antinomy is understood a pair of propositions, ap-

1. *Pu. R.* 269, *B* 410, 411.   2. *Pu. R.* 267, 268, *B* 406–9.

parently contradictory, which follow from the same set of assumptions. An antinomy is resolved either (a) by showing that the apparently contradictory propositions are in fact contradictories and follow from a certain internally inconsistent assumption, or (b) by showing that the apparently contradictory propositions are not in fact contradictory at all but mutually compatible. A trivial example of the first type of antinomy would be the propositions 'A square circle is round' and 'A square circle is not round'. It is resolved by showing that they follow from the self-contradictory assumption that a circle is square. A trivial example of the second type of antinomy is found in the apparently incompatible propositions 'The end of life is death' and 'The end of life is not death'. It is resolved by showing that 'end' is used for termination in the one case and for purpose in the other – two different senses.

An antinomy the source of which is hidden is particularly invidious and worrying. While other fallacies disguise from us the fallaciousness of our reasoning and may thereby give us a certain – however undeserved – peace of mind, antinomies the source of which is undiscovered incessantly remind us of our shortcomings as thinkers. Such are the cosmological antinomies which possess the highest degree of the salutary capacity 'to arouse philosophy from its dogmatic slumber and move it to the difficult business of the *critique* of reason itself'.[1] Kant believed that a popularization of his theory of knowledge might profitably begin by drawing attention to the antinomies of rational cosmology. This could be done, he says in a letter to Marcus Herz (11.5.1781), 'in a very flourishing style' and would excite 'the reader's desire to probe beneath the sources of this conflict'. But characteristically he adds that 'first *academic philosophy* (*die Schule*) must be given its due, only afterwards can one properly permit oneself to amuse the world'.

Within the limits of this Introduction I can do little more than reproduce the cosmological antinomies and show the method by which Kant resolves them. Once again, the cosmological antinomies are divided according to the table of the

1. *Prol.* 388.

Categories as – for so we might call them – the antinomies of quantity, of quality, of relation, and of modality respectively. *The first antinomy* has for its thesis: 'The world has a beginning in time and is also limited in space' and for its antithesis: 'The world has no temporal beginning and no limits in space; with respect to both time and space it is infinite.' *The second antinomy* has as its thesis: 'In the world every composite substance is composed of simple parts; nothing exists anywhere except it either is simple or is composed of simple parts' and as its antithesis, 'In the world no composite thing consists of simple parts and there exists nowhere in the world anything simple.'[1]

The third antinomy has as its thesis: 'Causality according to laws of nature is not the only kind of causality from which the phenomena of the world can be derived. It is necessary, in order to explain them, to assume a causality through freedom', i.e. to assume uncaused causes. Its antithesis is: 'There is no freedom; everything in the world takes place solely in accordance with laws of nature.' Lastly *the fourth antinomy* states as its thesis, 'There belongs to the world as a part of it or as its cause, something which exists as an absolute necessary being.' Its antithesis is, 'There exists nowhere an absolutely necessary being as the world's cause, either in it or out of it.'[2]

Each and every one of these conflicting propositions can be found among the central assumptions of one or more metaphysical systems. The first antinomy is relevant to any metaphysical theory which asserts or denies, explicitly or implicitly, that the world has been created at a point in time. The second is relevant to any metaphysical theory which asserts or denies the existence of atoms or monads of any kind. The third opposes determinism to indeterminism and thus indirectly, as Kant believes, opposes natural science to the foundation of ethics. The last antinomy expresses the conflict between metaphysical theories which try to prove and those which try to disprove the existence of God from premises about the world.

Kant insists that the proofs which he offers of each antithesis

1. *Pu. R.* 294, 295, and 301, 302, *B* 455 ff. and 462 ff.
2. *Pu. R.* 308, 309, and 314, 315, *B* 472 ff. and 480 ff.

and its thesis are not mere 'barristers' proofs' but are strictly valid. The proofs turn mainly on the nature of infinite aggregates. Their structure, since Kant's time, has been made the subject of an elaborate mathematical theory by Cantor and his successors. This does not mean that what Kant has to say on the matter is wholly superseded and belongs to the dark ages of logical superstition. Indeed Hilbert (in the paper quoted in ch. II, § 3) acknowledges his debt to Kant by saying expressly that he regards the notion of an infinite totality as a Kantian Idea of Reason.

On the other hand the Kantian arguments do seem to stand in need of modification in the light of developments in the logic of infinite aggregates subsequent to Cantor's work. To give one example: to Kant's assertion[1] that 'no aggregate is greatest' there corresponds a theorem in the modern theory of aggregates, but his reason for asserting it would now be rejected, namely that 'to every aggregate one or more units can be added'.[2] It is an express theorem that the addition of a finite number of units to an infinite aggregate does *not* increase its number. I cannot hold with any attempt to 'modernize' Kant's proofs of the antinomies. It would, as I think, end in mere idle speculations as to the sort of answer which Kant would have given to questions which simply could not have occurred to him.

Such speculations fortunately are not necessary for the understanding of Kant's main point about the cosmological antinomies. He sets about the demonstration that every single one of the cosmological *a priori* propositions, while claiming to be an absolute metaphysical truth, embodies a logical mistake. This demonstration, although prompted by the proofs of the antinomies, is not dependent for its validity on the correctness of these proofs.

The first antinomy concerns 'the magnitude of the world in space and time'. In stating that a volume of space or a stretch of time has a certain magnitude we assume that a process of measurement (the successive addition of units) can be com-

1. *Pu. R.* 296, *B* 458.   2. *Loc cit.*

pleted and *that its completion can be experienced*. Now the process of measuring the world in space and time cannot be completed in experience. The concept of its completion is thus an Idea to which nothing in experience can correspond. The statement that the world in space or time is finite or that it is infinite in magnitude is thus exactly similar to the statements that a square circle is round and that it is not round. Kant would probably not have been greatly disturbed by the claims of contemporary scientists to be able to estimate the magnitude of the world in space or time. He would merely have considered that the theorists were using concepts of measurement quite different from his.

The second antinomy concerns 'the division of appearances'. To the Idea of completing the unlimited division of a thing no experience can possibly correspond. The statement, however, that every substance consists of indivisible parts (or does not so consist) assumes that a process of division can be completed in experience which cannot in fact be so completed. Kant, here, is using the notion of a physical division which is assumed to be unlimited in principle – a division which, in particular, is not limited by available laboratory techniques or by the implications of a physical theory. The antinomies are contradictory pairs of absolute *metaphysical* propositions such as Democritus or Leibniz might have asserted, and not consequences of a physical theory based on experiment and observation.

In the first and second antinomies 'the falsity of the assumption consisted in that what contradicts itself in a concept (namely appearance as thing in itself) was presented as compatible'.[1] Indeed the idea of the completion of an unlimited process is that of a *non-phenomenon, intelligibile* or thing in itself. In the third and fourth antinomies 'the falsity of the assumption consists in that what is compatible is presented as incompatible'.[2]

The third antinomy concerns the question whether there is or is not freedom, i.e. are there or are there not uncaused causes? It is resolved by showing that the thesis – that all

1. *Prol.* 343.   2. *Loc. cit.*

phenomena are subject to 'causality according to laws of nature' – is compatible with the antithesis that a different kind of causality, allowing of uncaused causes, exists for *noumena* or things in themselves. The latter kind of causality is, of course, only an Idea – the Idea of freedom – which according to Kant is necessary to account for the experience of moral obligation. This experience is quite different from any objective experience which falls within the scope of the natural sciences, and is the theme of the *Critique of Practical Reason*.

The fourth antinomy concerns the existence or otherwise of an absolutely necessary being. Kant resolves it by distinguishing between a cause *within* the phenomenal world and an intelligible cause – a thing in itself – such as might be the cause *of* phenomena. The following two propositions are, then, compatible: the thesis that there is no absolutely necessary cause of the world of phenomena in accordance with laws of nature and the antithesis 'that this world is nevertheless connected with a necessary being as its cause (a different kind of cause and one according to a different law)'.[1]

Kant's resolution of the cosmological antinomies is evidence, if not of the truth, at least of the impressive logical force of the critical philosophy and of the theory of transcendental idealism as developed in Kant's Aesthetic and Analytic. The distinction between *phenomena* and *noumena* or the corresponding distinction, which to me seems preferable, between Ideas and other concepts helps to divest absolute metaphysics of its unlawful theoretical claims and prepares us for a recognition of the proper function of its Ideas and principles.

4. The Illusions of Speculative Theology

God, the subject of speculative theology, is conceived as an individual and the bearer of all possible perfections. A 'perfection' is not only a positive predicate into whose definition negation cannot enter; it is unlimited in the sense that it cannot

1. *Prol.* 347.

be incompatible with any other positive predicate. No empirical predicate, therefore, can be a perfection. Any positive empirical predicate, e.g. 'red' or 'square', is incompatible with some other such predicate, say 'green' or 'triangular'. The perfections of this most perfect being, or *ens realissimum* or God, can thus only be grasped 'by analogy'.

In assuming the applicability of an Idea of Reason (e.g. the soul conceived as the absolute unity of the thinking subject) we assume that an unlimited aggregate is given as completed. In assuming the existence of God we assume not only that the unlimited aggregate of all possible perfections is given as completed, but beyond this, that it applies to a single individual and that this individual is a person. Since the completion of an infinite aggregate cannot be an object of experience, the assumption that there is such an object is logically impossible. The thesis that God can be an object of experience, in the same sense in which objects which fall within the scope of natural science are, must therefore be rejected for the same reasons as the theses of speculative psychology and the theses and antitheses of speculative cosmology.

Yet just as the Ideas of the absolute unity of the thinking subject and of the absolute unity of the world may have a function and may even be necessary in our thinking about what ought to be and what is our duty, so the notion of God may have its proper and necessary place in moral thought. Notions to which nothing in objective experience can correspond can have no *direct* use in theoretical inquiries and their application after the fashion of *a posteriori* concepts and of the Categories must lead to confusion and fallacy. Yet our thinking about moral obligation cannot be limited to notions to which objective experience corresponds. This would be to equate what ought to be with what in fact is. The manner in which the notions of the soul, of freedom and of God are, according to Kant, connected with moral judgement is not, however, at present our concern.

Since the notion of God implies not only the completion of an infinite aggregate of predicates but also individuality and

indeed personality, Kant calls it not only an 'Idea', but also
an 'Ideal'. Since, unlike the notion of a perfectly wise *man* and
other such ideals, which – at least partly – are the result of the
imaginative combination of empirical concepts, the notion of
God contains no empirical element, Kant calls it 'the Ideal of
pure reason' or 'the transcendental Ideal'.

Although the concept of the existence of a bearer of all
possible perfections must be rejected as a possible object of
experience (it would be incompatible with the findings of the
Transcendental Analytic, which was the exposition of the concept 'object of experience') Kant still proceeds to consider the
main theoretical proofs for the existence of God which have
been put forward. These are the so-called ontological, cosmological and physico-theological arguments.

The ontological argument consists in an alleged deduction from
conceivability to existence; from the statement that a most
perfect being can be conceived to the statement that he exists.
The argument is intended as a *reductio ad absurdum*. If, it says,
there were a most perfect being who did not exist, there would
be a still more perfect being. There would be one who in addition to all the perfections of the former would have the added
perfection – the predicate of existence. A most perfect being
who does not exist is a contradiction in terms.

Kant's objection to this argument consists in pointing out
that 'existence' is not a predicate. 'Whatever, and however
much, our concept of an object contains [i.e. logically implies],
we must go beyond it in order to ascribe existence to it', that
is to say, in order to judge correctly that it is not empty. 'The
conception of a supreme being is in many respects a very useful Idea; because, however, it is a mere Idea, it is quite incapable by itself alone of extending our knowledge of that which
exists.'[1] Kant's objection can also be put in a slightly different
way. The premiss of the ontological argument states the fact
that we are capable of defining the notion of a supreme being.
The definition, like every definition, is formulated by an analytic statement. No analytic statement logically implies a

1. *Pu. R.* 402, 403, *B* 629.

synthetic statement. Yet the conclusion of the argument is synthetic.

The cosmological argument has as its premiss the synthetic statement that something exists, e.g., I myself do. It concludes – an equally synthetic statement – that an absolutely necessary being exists. Kant finds many logical flaws here. Perhaps the most fundamental is the assumption, the making of which in his view is the root of all the mistakes of absolute metaphysics, that an unlimited sequence (here a sequence of causes) is completable in experience. It is worth noting that the cosmological argument by itself does not prove the existence of God, but at most the existence of an absolutely necessary being.

The physico-theological argument or, as it is often called, the argument from design, has as its premiss a specific experience, namely that of apparent design. 'Everywhere do we see a chain of effects and causes, of ends and means, regularity in the way in which things come into being and cease to be',[1] and it is indeed very intelligible that we should feel inclined to conclude that there must be a creator or, at least, a builder of the world. Kant shows a certain tenderness for this argument, which has been fairly frequently propounded, even after the *Critique of Pure Reason* had become part of general philosophical education, and this by philosophers who clearly separated their religious from their philosophical convictions.[2] Yet an unlimited sequence of ends and means can, just as little as an unlimited sequence of causes and effects, be assumed to be completed in experience. In any case neither the argument from design nor the cosmological argument can prove the existence of the *ens realissimum*; since the former, if successful, would prove at most a world-builder, the latter at most an absolutely necessary being.

The fallacious character of the effort by the three theoretical arguments criticized to show that the Ideal of pure reason exists as an object of possible experience would not imply that no valid theoretical arguments existed unless the three argu-

1. *Pu. R.* 414, *B* 650.
2. E.g. Franz Brentano in *Vom Dasein Gottes*, Leipzig 1929.

F

ments really exhausted all the possibilities. But Kant believes himself to have shown this also. Whether or not he has done so hardly matters, inasmuch as the impossibility that the transcendental Ideal should be an object of experience is implied by the general principles of the Transcendental Logic.

On the other hand a theoretical disproof of the existence of a supreme being, i.e. a disproof of his existence as a *noumenon*, is, if we adopt Kant's position, equally impossible. Indeed 'the same grounds on which the inability of human reason to assert the existence [of a supreme being] has been demonstrated, are necessarily sufficient to demonstrate also the invalidity of any counter-assertion'.[1] Moreover, if *per impossibile* such a theoretical disproof could be given (one to the effect that God exists neither as a *phenomenon* nor as a *noumenon*) then the very proof of his existence on which Kant himself relies – his necessary existence as an Idea of *practical* reason – cannot, he believes, possibly be produced. Such a proof as this latter Kant himself believes possible, and produces in the *Critique of Practical Reason*.

5. The Legitimate Use of the Ideas of Pure Reason

The misuse of the Ideas to which nothing in experience can correspond consists in their spurious application to alleged objects of experience. It consists in using them after the fashion of *a posteriori* concepts which are applicable to experience because they are abstracted from it; or after the fashion of the Categories, which are applicable to experience because their applicability is a condition of there being objective experience, because, in other words, they are constitutive of objects.

Although the Ideas of reason cannot be applied to what is given in perception, they have in the field of theoretical thinking still an 'excellent and unavoidably necessary regulative use, namely to direct the understanding to a certain goal ... which serves the purpose of giving the greatest unity and the

1. *Pu. R.* 425, *B* 668.

greatest breadth at the same time'.[1] To understand this their legitimate function, we must recall the difference between the logical maxim of syllogistic ordering and the fundamental principle of pure reason (§ 1). The former enjoins us to ascend from premiss to premiss in a series of categorical, hypothetical, or disjunctive syllogisms, which has no last term. The latter demands that there be a last term and that the series be complete, and thus leads to the formation of the Ideas of the soul, the world, and God.

Thus far, it has not led to any of the mistakes of absolute metaphysics. These mistakes have their source in a further principle which might be called 'the fundamental principle of *dialectical* reason', namely that the series of conditions has a last term and is thus *complete in experience*. Only if we accept the last principle, which is very easily and naturally done, do we seem committed to the principles of absolute metaphysics.

If we only follow the logical maxim we achieve a progressive systematic ordering of our legitimate judgements. In Kant's representation of the matter we look for the *genus* of different species; for different *species* falling under the same genus; and for continuous transitions from one *species* to another. Kant calls these principles of ordering 'the principles of *homogeneity*, of *specification*, and of *affinity*'.[2] These principles are principles of ordering judgements and of classifying concepts. They are not themselves judgements and are not incompatible with each other since they can all be applied together 'up to a point'. In an analogous way a political society can be ordered by the interplay of the democratic, the aristocratic, and the monarchic principles.

Kant's maxim of syllogistic ordering is, of course, too restricted in scope – a result of his dependence on the traditional theory of deductive inference. We should recognize a much wider maxim of deductive ordering nowadays, the maxim which is conformed to when we systematize the results of scientific inquiry by means of so-called hypothetico-deductive systems. This type of deductive ordering differs from Kant's

1. *Pu. R.* 428, *B* 672.   2. *Pu. R.* 435, *B* 685.

syllogistic systematization in using many more types of deductive reasoning and in starting from axioms which for any given theory are regarded as being fundamental and not deducible from higher principles. Yet Kant's idea of a system of judgements is still recognizably similar to contemporary ideas of the systematic character of a scientific theory.

The Ideas of Reason themselves have also a further systematic or rather systematizing use if we consider them not as applicable in experience but rather as indicating unreachable goals which yet we can approximate; in other words if we use them as ideal standards, analogously to the way in which, in applied mathematics, limits are used which for various purposes it is sufficient to approximate to within this or that specified margin.

Thus in psychology it may be extremely useful 'to connect all appearances, actions and the receptivity of our mind … *as if* it were a simple substance, which endowed with personal identity (at least during life) permanently exists, while its states, to which those of the body belong only as external conditions, continuously change'.[1] In a similar way we may use the Idea of the totality of all things, or the world, or the Ideal of the *ens realissimum*. Far from being harmful this use of the Ideas may have not only great systematic but also great heuristic usefulness.

This 'as-if' justification of the Ideas of pure reason may be separated from the rest of the transcendental logic and elevated into a supreme maxim of method. We may decide in our theoretical endeavour to disregard the applicability or emptiness of concepts altogether and to employ only those which serve our purposes when treated *as if* they were applicable. We should then be methodological pragmatists. We might easily then be led to go further and consider the usefulness of a concept as the criterion of its applicability. Our pragmatism would then be epistemological or metaphysical. The writings of pragmatist philosophers often make it difficult to distinguish whether their pragmatism is merely methodological or something more.

1. *Pu. R.* 444, *B* 700.

What at first seems to be a pragmatist theory of truth or of the universe frequently turns out to be no more than the spirited proclamation of a methodological decree.

C. S. Peirce, one of the fathers of modern pragmatism, 'devoted two hours a day to the study of Kant's *Critique of Pure Reason* for more than three years until [he] almost knew the whole book by heart, and had critically examined every section of it . . .'[1] As a result of his study he rejects the arguments of the Analytic but finds a great deal that is worth while in the Dialectic. Kant, he says, subjects the Ideas of God, freedom, and immortality 'to a different kind of examination, and finally admits them upon grounds which appear to the seminarists more or less suspicious, but which in the eyes of the laboratorists are infinitely stronger than the grounds upon which he has accepted space, time, and causality'.[2]

It would be difficult to estimate how far Kant's philosophy of knowledge has 'influenced' Peirce. There can be no doubt in the case of Vaihinger's pragmatism in his *Philosophy of the As-If*. Vaihinger not only acknowledges his debt to the Transcendental Dialectic and other parts of Kant's critical philosophy but tries at great length to show how in his opinion it had anticipated his own variant of pragmatism.

The organized wealth of original and profound conceptions and of subtle analyses which is the *Critique of Pure Reason* contains, of course, the seeds of many modern philosophies. Concentration on the positive doctrine of the Dialectic to the exclusion of most other theses of the Kantian system leads, as we have seen, to pragmatism. Concentration on the doctrine of the Transcendental Logic as a whole to the exclusion of Kant's ethical works leads to a non-phenomenalist (non-Berkeleian) empiricism or positivism – provided the table of the Categories is not taken too literally. Twisting the Dialectic into a logic of truth leads to metaphysical systems of the Hegelian type. Even phenomenology and existentialism con-

1. *Selected Writings*, ed. Justus Buchler, p. 2.
2. *Loc. cit.* p. 16.

tain many recognizably Kantian elements. They certainly at least abound with Kantian terms.

The fundamental theses of the Kantian theory of knowledge are contained in the Transcendental Aesthetic, the Transcendental Logic and the Transcendental Dialectic which together form the first main part of the *Critique of Pure Reason* called the Transcendental Doctrine of Elements. Its second part, the Transcendental Doctrine of Methods, adds, as I believe, no important ideas which are both new and not to be found in Kant's later works – in particular the *Critique of Practical Reason*. A reader who has grasped the doctrine of the first part will find the second comparatively easy reading. For our purpose it is neither possible nor really necessary to consider it in any detail.

CHAPTER SIX

KANT'S ACCOUNT OF MORAL EXPERIENCE

1. The Conception of Practical Reason

REFLECTION upon our experience of moral obligation and moral conflict leads easily and naturally to the view that moral experience, although involving experience of impressions and objects, has important features of its own. If this general distinction holds good then the apparatus of concepts and principles, laid bare by the Transcendental Logic as conditions for the objectivity of one type of experience, may not be sufficient for a satisfactory account of moral experience which also claims to be in some sense objective. It is a new problem, and new, specifically moral concepts and principles have to be looked for, their claims examined, and their function investigated.

Indeed, to adopt the legal metaphor which Kant uses in the *Critique of Pure Reason*, we are 'in possession' of specifically moral concepts and specifically moral principles. Examples would be concepts such as 'duty' and principles such as 'inflicting pain for the mere sake of doing so is always wrong'. About the fact that we have such principles there is general agreement. There is no similar agreement about our right to them. Many have thought and many today hold that what seem to be moral principles are in truth empirical statements under a disguise, or definitions or merely expressions of an attitude. Others hold that man has been endowed with a special intuition or moral sense by which he is made aware of moral principles which are absolutely valid. The showrooms of the taxidermists of philosophy are full of dusty specimens of the species, 'Ethical Absolutism', 'Ethical Relativism', 'Ethical Intuitionism', 'Ethical Subjectivism', etc.

Ethical theories deduced from this or that dogma, which

happens to have proved itself useful in fields of experience which have nothing or little to do with morals, are mostly life-less. On the other hand, ethical theories developed too much in isolation from other branches of philosophical thinking are apt to be too naïve and simple to illuminate their subject matter. Kant's theory of ethics is remarkable in its comparative freedom from both these defects. It is always in the most intimate touch with moral experience and it is always developed in relation to the rest of his wide-ranging philosophical thought. Were it for no other reason but this, we could well expect to learn a great deal from the survey which he undertakes of our ethical 'possessions' and from his inquiry into their justifiability.

His theory – which is embodied mainly in the *Groundwork of the Metaphysic of Morals* (1785) and the *Critique of Practical Reason* (1788) – whatever its limitations, is at any rate no such philosophical afterthought as is suggested (in an essay on German philosophy) by the witty romantic poet and journalist Heinrich Heine. Kant's ethical theory provides, as we shall see, the grounds for what he calls 'a rational faith' in God. To Heine this possibility seems quite inconsistent with the spirit of the critical philosophy. He suggests that the author perhaps developed it to please his old manservant Lampe or to please the police; in any case for reasons which have little to do with philosophical convictions. They are indeed good enough reasons. After all 'old Lampe must have a God, else he cannot be happy, poor man', and the Prussian police like the existence of God for reasons which he elsewhere expounds[1] with much conviction. For 'whoever tears himself away from his God will sooner or later break with his earthly superiors too'. ('*Wer sich von seinem Gotte reisst, – wird endlich auch abtrünnig werden – Von seinen irdischen Behörden.*')

These – probably at least half-serious – remarks of Heine's about Kant's motives are, as I believe, rather specially unjustified in this particular case. Kant was never unduly afraid of his earthly superiors, who at one time forbade him all further pub-

1. *Memorials of Krähwinkel's days of terror.*

lication concerning religious questions. As to philosophical convictions, his theoretical philosophy is full of references to morality and religion. He indeed considers his transcendental idealism as the only firm foundation of an adequate theory of ethics and philosophy of religion, the only one which needs no sophistry to assist it.

The Critique of Pure Reason, which is concerned with our judgements of fact, is expressly aware that we also judge that certain things which are not fact, ought to be fact. Reason can be 'related in a twofold way to its object, either by merely *determining* it and its concept . . . or also by *making it real*'.[1] 'In the first function Reason is theoretical; in the second it is practical.'[2] Reason, and not the experience of impressions and objects, is the source of moral obligation (*das Sollen*). 'However many natural causes, however many sensory stimuli there may be, which drive me to *will* something, they cannot produce [my state of] *being under obligation* . . .'[3]

By speaking of reason as practical Kant wishes to indicate that our actions are not instigated or prevented, always and only, by desires and impulses; that we may decide to act or desist from acting on merely general principles and from no desire whatsoever. If we reflect upon our experience of inner conflict we can sometimes distinguish different types of it, according to the desires involved.

But there also occur conflicts which seem to differ from those, namely conflicts of desire *with duty*. If these, despite appearances, should turn out to be also conflicts merely between different desires, then we should have to agree that there is no practical reason. That reason can be practical means that what we call the opposition between reason and desire is the very opposition it seems to be.

It is important to remember once again here that Kant's terminology of faculties corresponds to distinctions between different types of experience and consequently to different types of proposition and types of concept and thus, in the end – if we are articulate enough – to different types of linguistic

1. *Pu. R.* 8, *B* ix.   2. *Loc. cit.*   3. *Pu. R.* 371, *B* 576.

expression and usage. There are occasions when it is advantageous to speak about differences of linguistic expression rather than differences in that about which we are talking. The present is not, as I believe, one of these occasions. The modern linguistic philosopher has not always the patience to learn to understand Kant's terminology. If we are to think of him and if we wish him not to miss what Kant has to say, we might perhaps explain to him the notion of practical reason by saying that for Kant the logical grammar of the term 'duty' is different from the grammar of 'desire' and 'impulse'; while yet the phrase 'conflict of duty with desire' is for him just as correct as the phrase 'conflict of one desire with another'.

The notions of a desire and of a conflict of desires are certainly susceptible of further analysis. Thus we often speak of desires when we should speak of long- or short-term dispositions. The problems which lead to this distinction[1] and the problems to which it leads in turn are not our concern here. The question for us is whether a notion of duty *not* abstracted from sense-experience and *not* involved in any principle of theoretical reason, is or is not spurious; and if not, what its function is, in thought and conduct. Our first task, therefore, must be a consideration of what we mean by stating about anything that it is 'our duty' (or, indeed, everybody's duty). In this context we might have selected any specifically moral notion for consideration instead of the notion 'duty', but I do not think that the examination of any other moral notion would lead us so naturally to the central problems of moral philosophy. In any case this was the opinion of Kant.

2. Duty, Maxims of Action, and the Moral Law

'It is impossible to conceive of anything in the world or out of it which can be considered good without qualification excepting only a *good will*.'[2] This famous and often quoted state-

1. See Ryle, *Concept of Mind*, London 1949.
2. *Gr.* 393, *Ab.* 9.

ment is the first sentence of the first section of the *Groundwork of the Metaphysic of Morals*. In this section Kant tries, as did Socrates before him, to elicit the ordinary man's view of morality in preparation for an inquiry into its conditions, its justifiability, and the modifications if any for which it may call.

To will is not to desire. It is to decide upon a course of action. Such a decision according to Kant is morally good only if it is taken *for the sake* of doing one's duty. This does not mean, as many readers of Kant's ethical works – including Friedrich Schiller – have believed, that a man who loves his neighbour cannot really do his duty by him. It does mean that we can do our duty without loving, and even whilst hating, humanity. Kant takes up Schiller's accusation that in his view dutiful action implies a hard and gloomy state of mind, and defends himself against it.

The defence is based on a distinction between duty and virtue. Virtue is the firmly rooted disposition to perform one's duty. And, says Kant, 'If we ask: What is the *aesthetic* character of virtue – so to speak its *temperament* – is it courageous and so joyous, or anxious and depressed? Then an answer is hardly necessary.'[1]

Sir David Ross and others following him have understood Kant as defining 'it is my duty to do act *A*' to mean the same as 'it is my duty to do act *A* from the sense that it is my duty to do act *A*'.[2] To this they object first that if it is my duty to do act *A* simply it cannot also be my duty to do act *A* from the sense of duty; and secondly that the definition leads to an infinite regress, since the notion of duty is defined in terms of itself.

The objections against this definition are justified, but the definition is not Kant's. Kant is merely showing that in using the notion of duty, even before philosophizing about it, we often distinguish between actions which externally conform to duty (*pflichtmässige Handlungen*) and actions done for the sake of

1. *Rel.* 23, footnote.
2. *The Right and the Good*, Oxford, 1930, p. 5.

or from duty (*Handlungen aus Pflicht*). For Kant the distinction
is no more than a step towards the clarification of the notion
of duty. It raises the question as to what is and what is not
required for regarding an action as moral apart from considering it as a piece of observable conduct. There is thus nothing
illogical in the distinction. Moreover, Kant is merely considering a common view in a preliminary way. Indeed the section
of the *Groundwork* in which he is doing this is entitled 'Transition from the common moral knowledge to the philosophical'.

Kant's conception of a moral decision as a decision which is
taken not merely *in accordance with* duty but *for the sake of* it does
not require that the complex of motives which notoriously
vexes us when we ask ourselves *why* we did such and such an
action, or *why* we took such and such a decision, should be
capable, always, of being disentangled. That we have a concept of duty does not mean that we are sure to apply it correctly in actual situations. All that is being claimed by the
Kantian theory is that in certain simplified typical circumstances we know what it would be like to do our duty. The
concept of duty is in this respect not different from that of a
chemically pure substance or other similar concepts in the
natural sciences.

If we wish to find out whether or not an action on a given
occasion was done *for the sake of* duty, it does not help merely
to know the doer's intention – the state of affairs which he
intended to bring about. Neither will it help to know the
consequences of his action. Clearly an action intended to bring
about a given state of affairs and followed by a given chain of
consequences *may* have been done for the sake of duty; but
again it may not.

According to Kant the moral value of the action lies '*in the
maxim* according to which it has been decided upon'.[1] 'A
maxim is', he explains, 'the subjective principle of action ...',
that is to say, 'the principle according to which the subject *is
acting*', not the objective principle according to which he
ought to act.[2] It is, of course, possible that the doer's maxim may

1. *Gr.* 399, *Ab.* 16.   2. *Gr.* 421, *Ab.* 38, footnote.

conform to the moral law just as it is possible that his maxim
or maxims should be incompatible with it.

A person's maxim is a general rule which he chooses to follow in his actions. His adopting it implies that he intends to
conform to it. It does not imply that he always will in fact so
conform. We all have maxims which, sometimes at least, we
violate. These are by no means confined to morality. They may
concern any kind of activity as long as it makes sense to say
that they can be satisfied or violated by an action.

To say that we act in accordance with a maxim is not to
imply that before or during the action we necessarily 'say it
over' to ourselves; or that we bring it consciously to our
notice at all. On occasion, we may. If, for example, some highly
irascible person adopts the maxim to suppress the outbursts of
temper he is likely to say it over to himself when trying to act
on it. At the other extreme there are the border-line cases in
which it may be difficult to distinguish acting upon a maxim
(or in violation of one) from a piece of purely automatic behaviour. Such border-line cases are themselves evidence that
we adopt maxims for our actions even if we formulate them
only rarely. They are formulated and become clearly conscious
as a rule only when we are called upon, or when we call upon
ourselves, to justify our actions; or again if maxims are im-
puted to us which we have not in fact adopted.

It is impossible, by considering an action merely by itself, to
determine the maxim according to which it was done. The
same action could accord with or violate many maxims – different and even mutually incompatible ones. The hackneyed
example of the text-books, the action of subscribing a sum of
money to a charity, illustrates the point. The maxim in conformity with which this act was done might be to help those
in need whenever possible, or to take every opportunity of
becoming known as a public benefactor, or even to devote one's
illicit gambling gains always to a good object, and so on.

The maxim of a particular action is *not* the decision to perform it. It is the rule which the doer has adopted and to which,
in deciding as he does, he conforms. To know a person's

maxim is to know what *he has included* in it, or 'what he has made the general rule in accordance with which he wishes to behave'.[1] To choose maxims is to choose a policy. A maxim may be simple such as, for example, 'not to tell a lie under any circumstances', or 'to lie only when one can be reasonably sure of not being found out'. It may also be very complex. If it is so overgrown with qualifications that no action can in fact conform to it, we should not call it a maxim; if only one action can, we should, at least, hesitate to call it so; while a self-contradictory rule could not be a maxim at all, since every action would both conform to it and violate it. Normally a maxim is such that many actions, even an unlimited number, can correspond to it.

'Everything in nature acts in accordance with laws. Only a rational being has the ability to *act according to the presentation* [*Vorstellung*] of laws, i.e. according to principles . . .'[2] In other words only a being who is capable of adopting maxims can be moral or immoral. No being not capable of this – an amoeba, a tiger, certain mental defectives – can be either. Such a being is a-moral.

A maxim is moral if it accords with the moral law – provided, of course, that there is such a law. From what has been said before, the morality of an action does not lie in the desires and purposes of the doer or in its consequences. The morality of an action, Kant concludes, is therefore nothing but its 'conformity to law in general' [*die allgemeine Gesetzmässigkeit der Handlungen überhaupt*].[3] My action, Kant explains, is moral if, and only if, '*I can also will that my maxim should become a universal law*'.[4]

There can be little doubt that Kant's principle, whether or not it is, as Kant believes, the ultimate principle of morals, is highly relevant to the way in which we judge of the morality of actions. We do most certainly condemn as immoral a person who at one and the same time wills that a certain rule be universally adopted and omits to follow it himself – the person

1. *Rel.* 24.   2. *Gr.* 412, *Ab.* 29.   3. *Gr.* 402, *Ab.* 18.
4. *Loc. cit.*

who defends general conscription, for example, and himself tries to escape it, the person who preaches water and himself drinks wine, the black-marketeer who makes profits from the violation of a law whose observance by other people is the condition of his gains.

We can accept all this without committing ourselves to the type of ethical absolutism which would hold that an action either is absolutely moral or is absolutely not moral; that, in particular, differences merely in the person of the doer have no relevance to the question. Nor do we commit ourselves thereby to the view that Kant's principle is a necessary and sufficient test of the morality of an action. On the other hand, it has to be admitted that he himself holds both these views. Before discussing them, however, more must be said about his conception of the function of this 'absolute' principle.

First of all, it is not a maxim. It is a test which is applicable to all maxims, without ambiguity. Every action conforms to or violates the doer's maxims, and the maxims themselves conform to or violate the moral principle. An action can conform to the moral principle but only indirectly, i.e. *via* the maxim. If we are given a detailed description of a person's action *without* being given the maxim, we are not in a position to pass a moral judgement. On the other hand, the application of the principle to a maxim does not add anything to the content or matter of it; it only permits us to make a moral judgement about it. This is why, in the theoretical sphere, the principles by which we determine whether a syllogism is or is not valid are also regarded as formal; it is because they add nothing to the content of its premisses or conclusion or to the relation in which these stand to each other. Just as the formal principles of syllogistic reasoning divide all syllogisms clearly into two classes, the valid and the invalid, so, Kant believes, the formal principle of morality divides all maxims, and consequently all actions based on them, into those which are moral and those which are not.

We can imagine a being so constituted as always to be able to act purely on moral maxims and who would never be sub-

ject to an inclination toward actions not based on them. Such
a being would be what Kant calls 'holy' and have a holy will.
Man cannot reach this ideal. He will always feel disposed towards wrong actions in some cases at least and will then experience the conflict between desire and duty. He will try to
impose upon himself, without or with success, maxims which
conform to the formal principle of morality. Imposed rules are
imperatives. Men, unlike holy beings, will apprehend the formal
principle of morality always as an imperative. The imperative
of duty, the command to us to do our duty and to do it for its
own sake, depends, as we shall see presently, on no condition.
It does not tell us 'Do your duty *if* this or *unless* that ...' It is
categorical.

3. The Categorical Imperative as the Test of Morality

This categorical imperative, as which we human beings apprehend the formal principle of morality, admits, according to
Kant, of a number of formulations. The first is (in Paton's
translation): 'Act only on that maxim through which you can
at the same time will that it should become a universal law.'
Since all effects happen in accordance with laws of nature, the
categorical imperative can also be formulated: 'Act as if the
maxim of your action were to become through your will a
universal law of nature.'

Both formulations are clear and exhibit the contrast between
the categorical imperative and conditional or hypothetical
ones. Kant distinguishes between 'rules of skill' and 'counsels
of prudence'.[1] A counsel of prudence would take the form:
'*If* under the given circumstances you want to achieve the
greatest possible happiness then you must etc. ...' A rule of
skill would take the form: '*If* under the given circumstances
you want to achieve a certain specific purpose, other than or as
well as happiness, then you must etc. ...' Hypothetical imperatives are really statements about the course of nature. The

1. *Gr.* 416, *Ab.* 33.

statement 'If you want an event B, or an event of type B, to happen, then you must bring about an event A or of type A' says no more than 'A is the only cause of B and it is in your power to bring A about.'

We return now to Kant's claim that the application of the categorical imperative to maxims enables us to draw an absolute distinction between those which are moral and those which are not. The distinction is supposed to be absolute in the sense that it does not depend on the person who adopts it. It will be best, I think, to start with Kant's own examples in order to grasp his position.

His first example is the case of a suicide who has been acting on the principle 'from self-love to shorten life if ... it threatens more evil than it promises pleasantness'.[1] Now, Kant argues, the conception of an order of nature in which such a maxim were a universal law would contradict itself. In other words, by the application of the categorical imperative the maxim is shown not to be moral. The action based on it will be wrong.

Next Kant takes the maxim on which a person was acting, who, finding himself in financial straits, reflects as follows: 'If I believe myself short of money, I will borrow money and promise to pay it back, although I know that this will never happen.'[2] If this maxim were to be elevated into a universal law such promises and the purpose which they serve would become impossible. So, once again, the maxim is not moral.

The third example is the maxim of a gifted pleasure-seeker who neglects the cultivation of his gifts for the sake of pleasure. His maxim again is not moral. Neglecting one's natural gifts for the sake of pleasure is, so Kant argues, incompatible with the conception of a rational being and therefore could not become a law of nature. Kant's last, and to my mind least convincing example, is the maxim neither to help others in distress nor require anybody's help if one is oneself in distress. Once more, the maxim is not moral, he says, since nobody can *will* this to become a universal law of nature. He would thereby

1. *Gr.* 422, *Ab.* 39.   2. *Loc. cit.*

G

'deprive himself of all hope of the support which he himself desires'.[1]

This procedure of testing the morality or otherwise of a maxim by applying the formal principle of morality consists always in finding out whether one can will the maxim to become a universal law of nature. A maxim, so tested, either leads to a contradiction or it does not. In the one case the maxim will not conform to the categorical imperative, in the other it will. There is, Kant holds, no third possibility. Moreover, there is only one way in which any given maxim can be made into a universal law.

From these examples, especially the third and fourth, it is quite clear that Kant's test-procedure does not consist merely in first replacing the 'I' of the maxim by 'everybody', and then seeing whether the resulting universal law is logically self-contradictory. In the third and fourth examples and even, I should add, in the first and second, the universalized maxims are not logical contradictions. What Kant says about the application of the categorical imperative together with his illustrations seems to admit of three possible interpretations.

We might first extend the notion of contradiction or absurdity to cover not only logical impossibility, but also another type of absurdity which we might call 'moral'. This interpretation would bring Kant's position very near to that of contemporary intuitionists, for example G. E. Moore or Sir David Ross, and, in spite of Kant's emphatic disclaimer,[2] to that of their predecessors the English moral-sense school, e.g., Shaftesbury, who was widely read in Kant's time and very highly thought of by him. If we take the position that a *moral* absurdity is something apprehended by a specific moral sense, then Kant's test clearly becomes circular – or else superfluous. His view would then even show some slight similarity to Hobbes's ethical teaching, to which in other respects it is diametrically opposed. According to Hobbes[3] '*injustice*, in the controversies of the world, is somewhat like to that, which in

1. *Gr.* 423, *Ab.* 41.   2. *Gr.* 442, *Ab.* 60 ff.
3. *Leviathan*, Pt. 1, chap. 14.

the disputations of the scholars is called absurdity. For as it is here called an absurdity, to contradict what one maintained in the beginning: so in the world, it is called injustice, and injury, voluntarily to undo that, which from the beginning, he had voluntarily done.' It must be noted that Kant[1] makes an express point of distinguishing between self-contradictory thoughts and self-contradictory acts of willing.

According to another interpretation Kant's test-procedure consists not in finding out whether the universalized maxim by itself is contradictory, but whether it *in conjunction with other true statements about the world* is logically impossible. The difficulty of this interpretation lies in the question which statements about the world are to be considered in order to judge of the morality of an action. Some of them would have to be empirical statements whose truth might be doubtful. In particular Kant's fourth example of an immoral maxim can be shown to be immoral only if we make certain assumptions about the psychological make-up of human beings and indeed of all rational beings.

The third possible interpretation is a combination of the first and the second. We might extend the notion of absurdity to cover both. Of the three it seems to me that Kant's examples point on the whole to the second interpretation, while his conception of practical reason, and practical validity, as opposed to theoretical reason and theoretical truth, points to the first. In this case we should have to admit that his theory is embarrassed by the difficulties of both interpretations.

We have seen that 'conformity to law in general' ranks with Kant as the necessary and sufficient condition of the morality of maxims and through them of actions. The conception recalls to some extent Rousseau's notion of the general will. Kant admired Rousseau and may well have been influenced by his social and moral philosophy. It seems as if he had subjected Rousseau's stimulating but vague and self-contradictory theory of the general will as the morally good will, to a thorough examination and purification.

1. *Gr.* 424, *Ab.* 41.

Rousseau's doctrine of the connexion between the morality and the generality of a law is concentrated in the following passage from one of his works:[1] 'The body politic is also a moral being, possessed of a will, and this general will tends always to the preservation and welfare of the whole and every part ... and constitutes for all the members of the state ... the rule of what is just and unjust.' The great difficulty of this doctrine lies in the fact that the machinery which in any given community expresses the general and therefore the good will may miscarry and ordain immoral laws. This possibility is admitted by Rousseau, who therefore distinguishes between the *general will*, which is necessarily moral, and the so-called *will of all*, which may not be. But Rousseau gives us no independent criterion by which we may distinguish whether a given principle expresses the general will or only the will of all. He gives us no criterion of the morality of principles, and therefore none of the morality of actions.

Kant's test for judging of maxims has difficulties implicit in it, if interpreted in any of the three ways just mentioned. But even if the difficulties could not be avoided, his formal principle would remain, I believe, extremely important for the understanding of moral experience and moral judgement. It is first of all in many cases a clear test of wrongness: a person whose acts violate a principle which he wills to be a universal law is acting wrongly. Moreover, if, unlike Kant, we admit the possibility of alternative moral codes, the principle helps us to distinguish moral codes from a-moral codes of behaviour, i.e. from those which, like codes of fashion, have nothing to do with morality. Unless a code of rules contains the formal principle of morality, it is not a moral code.

A Kantian, however, could *not* admit, e.g., that a moral code which prescribed polygamy and one which prescribed monogamy were genuine alternatives in the sense that either of the two incompatible maxims, that of polygamy and that of monogamy (though not both together) could stand Kant's test; that it could without absurdity, logical or moral, be willed to be-

1. *Discours sur l'Économie Politique,* Bibliothèque de la Pléiade, Vol. III, p. 244.

come universal law. He would have to hold, it seems, either
that one of the maxims was immoral; or else that the two
maxims were not really incompatible because we would find,
if we considered them carefully, that they included a reference to a set of social conditions which was different in each
case.

Both lines of argument involve the difficulties we raised in
interpreting Kant's test-procedure, and neither of the two
seems to me convincing. It is clear, however, that a person
who wills monogamy to become a universal law and adopts
polygamy as his own maxim is immoral. It is equally clear that
the principles of polygamy or monogamy are moral principles
only if they belong to a system of rules which contains the
formal principle of morality.

Kant has, I believe, shown that the formal principle of
morality must be contained in every code of rules which can
profess to be a moral code as distinguished from an a-moral
one. He claims to have shown much more: namely that no two
codes containing the principle can be incompatible, that is to
say, there is really only *one* moral code. What conforms to it is
moral for all rational beings and what violates it is immoral for
all rational beings.

We may note two points before continuing the exposition.
First, the difference between one who admits the possibility of
alternative, equally valid, moral codes and one who does not
admit it, is much smaller in practice than in theory. The principles which are in fact adopted are in many cases identical.
Also a person who has adopted a moral code may adhere to it
just as strictly whether he believes that it does or does not
admit of alternatives; and the belief that there may be genu-
inely alternative moral codes must not be confused with the
belief that moral judgements have no meaning. Secondly, just
as the person who admits the possibility of other systems of
physics besides the Newtonian may still learn a great deal from
Kant's theoretical philosophy, so the person who believes in
the possibility of more than one system of morals has a great
deal to learn from Kant's practical philosophy even although,

in both cases alike, only one system is acknowledged as
possible by Kant himself.

4. Can the Categorical Imperative be Objective?

The notion of duty, Kant has argued, involves the categorical
imperative. More precisely, if, in any action, one has done
one's duty, then the maxim of the action has conformed to the
formal principle of morality; and the statement also holds in
reverse: if there has been this conformity then one has not
violated one's duty. To unravel the content of a concept is,
of course, to demonstrate neither the applicability of it nor the
truth (the objectivity) of any of the principles which we have
uncovered in the process. Kant himself quite emphatically
states that the analysis of the conception of duty does not, and
cannot, prove 'that there is a practical law which by itself
commands absolutely and independently of all motives, and
that to observe this law is duty'.[1]

Philosophical reflection often leads to the question whether
an entity is real, or a principle objective. Because of an almost
hopeless instability in the use of the term 'objective' the question is often confused and confusing. 'Objectivity' is used in
completely different senses and often with no clear meaning at
all. Before asking whether a principle is objective, or looking
for an answer to the question, one should know under what
conditions the answer would be affirmative. Without this our
interrogative sentence does not express a question. It only
expresses puzzlement, uneasiness, the suspicion that perhaps
there is a problem here. Such perplexity, while it is the beginning of most, perhaps all, philosophical inquiry, is not itself
the formulation of a problem.

What question then are we asking when we ask whether the
categorical imperative is objective; and what are the conditions
under which our answer would have to be affirmative? It is
clear that the objectivity or, if we like, the absolute validity of

1. *Gr.* 425, *Ab.* 43.

the categorical imperative must be different from the objectivity of the synthetic *a priori* principles which are the conditions of the experience of physical objects and of science. The categorical imperative does not, whatever else its function may be, confer objectivity on perceptual judgements. The apprehension of it and the 'feeling' of respect for the law which accompanies it may conflict with desires which can be described by perceptual judgements. But it modifies neither these desires nor their description.

The conditions under which the categorical imperative would have to be regarded as objective are made quite clear by Kant, and thereby the meaning of practical as opposed to theoretical objectivity. He demands that a connexion between the concept of 'a rational being in general' and the adoption by such a one of the categorical imperative be proved.[1] He demands further that this connexion be proved to be *synthetic*: for, obviously, if we define a rational will as one which adopts the categorical imperative we remain within the field of conceptual analysis, where we can do no more than uncover the logical content of concepts – an activity which is pointless if it immediately follows an explicit definition. There would be no point in first defining the rational will as a will subject to the categorical imperative, and then pronouncing that every rational will must be subject to it. That would be like putting a book into a drawer and then, with a gesture of surprise, taking it out again.

The connexion must further be proved to be *a priori*. To show that all rational beings are, as a matter of fact, subject to the categorical imperative would not be enough. To prove the objectivity of the categorical imperative is to prove that they *must* be subject to it. Now the 'must' in question cannot be that of analytic connexion, since the connexion has been required to be synthetic. The only kind of necessary propositions which are not analytic are, according to the Kantian classification of propositions,[2] synthetic *a priori* propositions. In other words, to prove the objectivity of the categorical imperative

1. *Gr.* 426, *Ab.* 44.   2. Ch. 1, §§ 2, 3.

is to prove, at least, the *synthetic a priori* character of the proposition that the will of every rational being is subject to the
categorical imperative.

Even this demand, however, stands in need of further qualification – a point which becomes obvious at once when we
recall that Kant held the Transcendental Analytic to contain a
complete list of all (theoretical) synthetic *a priori* principles. In
other words we must prove that our synthetic *a priori* connexion does not belong with those in the previous list but is of
a special kind – that it is a *practical* synthetic *a priori* principle,
i.e. one which can determine our will independently of and
even in opposition to our desires.

Kant insists that a will which is subject to the categorical
imperative, whether it obeys it or not, need not necessarily be
a human rational will. The will of any rational being is so
subject. His point here is that while a human will can be determined by both the categorical imperative and by desires,
the latter determination has nothing to do with the connexion
between the notion of a rational will and that of its being subject to the categorical imperative. What is true of man *qua*
rational must be true of all beings who are rational however
different they may be from man in other respects. Kant is not
concerned with the question whether such beings exist. His
emphasis on rational beings in general in this connexion serves
a purely logical purpose. It is, so I believe, no more a faint
echo of medieval discussions about the nature of angels than it
is a prophetic allusion to the arrival, in flying saucers, of rational but not human beings from outer space.

A proposition is synthetic, as we saw, if its negation is not
a contradiction in terms. It is *a priori* if it is logically independent of any proposition which describes sense-impressions.
Now the proposition that a rational will is subject to the
categorical imperative can be, and often is, denied without
self-contradiction. It is also independent of all propositions
describing sense-impressions. With this, at least, all empiricist
philosophers would readily agree. The proposition under consideration is thus synthetic *a priori*.

To say this, however, is to say very little and certainly not all that Kant wishes to say. It is, we remember, a characteristic of all synthetic *a priori* propositions that they are necessary, and that the necessity (see ch. I) is not the logical necessity of analytic propositions. In the case of synthetic *a priori* propositions which are theoretical it consists in their being conditions of our thinking about matters of fact and, as the *Critique of Pure Reason* has shown, of the experience of objects. In the case of the categorical imperative the necessity consists in its relevance to a different region of experience and thought – namely moral experience and moral judgement. It is practical, i.e. it can determine the will.

Kant's question whether the categorical imperative is an objective principle thus becomes clear. We know now that to demonstrate it is to show that the statement 'The will of a rational being is subject to the categorical imperative' is synthetic, is *a priori*, and is practically necessary. Its synthetic and *a priori* character can be, and has been, demonstrated. Has it, however, practical necessity, that is to say, can the categorical imperative determine the will?

An answer to this question is not easy to find. Indeed it is not at all easy to see even how the categorical imperative could *possibly* determine the will. If we set ourselves a purpose we depend on our desires and not on our rationality: for it is not absurd to assume that there are rational beings whose desires are quite different from ours and who, consequently, would set themselves altogether different purposes or ends for their actions. Our subjection *qua* rational beings to the categorical imperative cannot be explained in terms of our seeking ends which depend on our desires. This difficulty, Kant argues, can be overcome. 'Assuming that there exists something *the existence of which* in itself has objective value, that is to say, something which *as an end in itself* could be the ground of determinate laws, then in it and only in it would lie the ground of a possible categorical imperative, that is of a practical law.'[1] In other words, if it can be shown that there is an end in itself or

1. *Gr.* 428, *Ab.* 46.

an end which is independent of any kind of desire, then the
law to the effect that this end should be pursued would be
binding for every rational will.

At this point Kant introduces a postulate: 'Man and every
rational being *exists* as end in itself, *not merely as means* for arbitrary use by this will or that; but he must in all his actions
... be regarded *at the same time as an end*.'[1] We shall find it
necessary for justification of the postulate eventually to step
outside the confines of moral experience and make use of some
results arrived at in the *Critique of Pure Reason*. For the present
we must be content with an explanation of the postulate, especially of its key-notion, 'man as an end in himself'.

Kant's conception of an end in itself must be distinguished
from the ordinary or, as we may say, relative notion of end and
means. A thing, a person, or a state of affairs is a means or an
end only in relation to some plan or policy which is either pro-
jected or put into practice. A state of affairs is a means in so far
as it is a condition for bringing about some other state of
affairs. A thing or a person is a means, by having a certain
function in some state of affairs – we might say, roughly speaking, in so far as it is used as a tool. A state of affairs is an end
in so far as, in the framework of a given policy, it is to be
brought about without itself being a means to some further
end.

A policy is a hierarchy of means and ends or a system of such
hierarchies. Apart from its place in a policy every such hierarchy is part of a causal chain. Consider the simple example: A
the means to B, B the means to C. Here A, B, C must be links
in a causal chain in which A has an infinite number of causal
antecedents and C an infinite number of causal consequents.
The hierarchy has a first member (A) and a last member (C);
the causal sequence of which it is a part has neither beginning
nor end.

When Kant says that man, or any rational being, is an end
in himself (an absolute end) he means that in *some sense* man
stands outside all causal chains and consequently outside every

1. *Loc. cit.*

hierarchy of means and ends. In treating man as a means only, we ignore part of his nature – his being a rational being, a person, an end in itself. We think of ourselves as persons, i.e. as at least beings who claim to be able to function otherwise than merely as tools or means in the policy of *another person*. The recognition of our own personality thus implies the recognition of other persons, that is to say beings who are policy makers and who claim not to be used as mere tools. We all make this claim; and we could not make it if we regarded ourselves as being *wholly immersed* in causal chains. For to be a tool is to function in certain ways in a causally necessary state of affairs which someone, as a matter of fact, happens to desire.

5. The Autonomy of the Will

A further important formulation of the categorical imperative is obtained if we assume as a postulate that 'rational nature exists as an end in itself'. We can then say: 'Act in such a way that you treat humanity, both in your own person and in the person of all others, never as a means only but always equally as an end.'[1] Kant is not very clear how, exactly, this postulate, in conjunction with the original formula of the categorical imperative, leads to the new formulation. It is hardly a case of logical deduction.

The connexion seems to be somewhat as follows: once we assume this postulate, we can adopt a great variety of maxims about treating men as means only or treating them also as ends. We might, for example, make their treatment as ends conditional upon such considerations as how they earn their living or how they dress or the colour of their skins. The new formula which conforms to the categorical imperative as originally formulated would be found as one amongst these maxims. But the new formula covers all the situations which are covered by the old one. Moreover an action or maxim which is morally good according to the old formula is morally

1. *Gr.* 429, *Ab.* 47.

good according to the new one and *vice versa*. Consequently the difference between the two formulas is only one of formulation and not of function. Kant illustrates this point by using the new formula to test the same maxims which he tested by the old one – with the same result.

Although the new formulation of the categorical imperative can be obtained only by the help of the postulate, so far unjustified, that rational beings are ends in themselves, it does, so I believe, correspond to moral experience, at least to moral experience in our culture, as we find that expressed not only in 'commonsense' moral judgements, but in countless works of moral and social philosophy, works of art, and expressions of religious belief. Even the tyrants, of whom there have been enough in our civilization, may be found paying lip-service to the categorical imperative when they claim, however hypocritically, that they do not treat their subjects as mere means.

Recognition of the principle that man is an end in himself is shown very clearly in the need which has habitually been felt to explain away all exploitation of man by man. Thus in the case of slavery Aristotle tries to justify the institution by introducing the conception of natural slaves, i.e. slaves who are men but not also rational beings. He has to admit, however, that in his society many are slaves who are not slaves by nature. His uneasiness is quite obvious.[1] His arguments and waverings point clearly to the fact that he is somehow aware of the principle that men should not be treated as means only. The same truth comes to light in the tortuous arguments by which people have tried to justify child labour, racial and political persecution, and the notorious doctrine that 'the end justifies the means'.

Man as a rational being experiences the formal principle of morality as a categorical imperative. If he were wholly governed by causal necessity he could not determine his own will in accordance with it. He might possibly experience the conflict between duty and desire, but he would not have the power to do his duty in opposition to desires. These alone would

1. See *Politics*, Bk. I, ch. VI.

determine all his actions. Moreover, he could not conceive of any general principles to be followed except such as commended certain relative ends.

A moral principle which is to be independent of all desires and the purposes to which they give rise, must, Kant holds, have its source outside all causal chains. Man in so far as he is a rational being (and, therefore, *any* rational being, whatever his desiring nature) must be taken as its source. Rational beings are thus not only subject to the categorical imperative but are also the creators of it. In other words, every rational being is not only subject with respect to the moral law; he is also legislator. We thus arrive at the '*Idea of the will of any* rational being as a universally legislative will.'[1]

This *Idea* again agrees well with our conception of a morally good action, an action done for the sake of duty. An action which is done merely in order to conform to some external law, is for that very reason not done for the sake of duty. To act for the sake of duty is to act in order to conform to a *self-imposed* law, which may, but need not, have the same content as some external law. At times a person may be able to perform a morally good action only if he does it in defiance of some external law of his community. Actions conforming to these laws may be immoral. As the metaphor goes, the 'voice' of duty or of conscience is an inner voice. Even the person who believes the laws he is following to be God's commandments must first of all recognize the following of them as his duty.

The fact of our observing self-imposed laws in acting for the sake of duty, and so being subjects and legislators at the same time, does, of course, not mean that we are doing our duty for its own sake. We may as easily be mistaken about our duty as about matters of fact. We may impose on ourselves wrong laws – laws which do not conform to the categorical imperative. Where there is the possibility of universally valid (objective) principles, there is also the possibility of error. This holds as much in the sphere of practical reason as of theoretical.

1. *Gr.* 431, *Ab.* 49.

The conception of man as both subject and author of his laws lies at the basis of a great deal of Western political thought. In particular all so-called consent-theories of political obligation argue that man ought to, and that he sometimes in fact does, live under self-imposed laws. Even defenders of absolute government, such as the later Roman lawyers or Hobbes, consider the citizens of the community as only having delegated their legislative power by a real or hypothetical contract. Rousseau's doctrine is that the general will of the community is the real moral will of all its members, which again clearly presupposes that if the citizens' political obligations are to be moral obligations they must in some way be self-imposed. All these political theories show a dim awareness of Kant's conception that the rational will is subject to its own legislation. It is, however, often obscured by ambiguities, by special pleading, and often by a too narrow concern with purely political issues to the exclusion of the wider questions of philosophy.

Kant describes as 'heteronomy' the assumption that the will of a rational being is subject to moral laws or principles, *not* the result of its own legislation *qua* rational will. In it he sees the root of the unsatisfactory state in which he found the theory of morals. In the *Critique of Practical Reason* he gives a list of six types of moral theory which teach that the determinant of the will is either an empirical state of affairs or an Idea of reason, and not its own legislation. Of the empirical theories he cites that of Montaigne, according to whom the principles of morality are determined by education; that of Mandeville, according to which they are determined by the legal system; that of Epicurus, who sees the ground of morality in physical pleasure; and that of Hutcheson, who sees it in moral feeling. Of those heteronomous moral theories which regard an Idea of reason as the ground of morality he mentions the theory, held by the Stoics and Wolff, that morality is based on the Idea of inner perfection, and the theory, held by Crusius and the theological moralists, that it is based on the will of God. All these theories admit of many variations. They have been put forward time and again in different shapes, and it seems safe to predict that many books in many languages will still be written in which they are propounded again by writers assuming the air of discoverers of new and uncharted territory.

Kant's rejection of these theories need not imply their irrelevance to morals. Indeed education, the legal system, physical and 'moral' feelings, reflection on the idea of perfection in general, and religious experience may all occasion us to become aware of the formal principle of morality and its relation to the will. In a similar manner experience of facts occasions us to apprehend theoretical principles. In both alike, however, the occasion of awareness of *a priori* principles must not be confused with the source from which these principles themselves are derived. While they may, according to Kant, be brought to our minds by, or while they may be made to occur to us upon the occasion of, experience, they are not on this account to be regarded as derived from experience by abstraction.

CHAPTER SEVEN

The Possibility of Moral Experience and its Relation to Science and Religion

1. Moral Freedom and Natural Necessity

IF the experience of conflict between duty and desire is not an illusion; if the judge's familiar references to criminal responsibility are more than indirect ways of describing the necessary course of events; if man is subject to a self-imposed moral law; then we must assume that man exists not only as a part of the causal order of nature, but also outside it. We must assume that he is an end in himself, that he is morally free.

Before turning to Kant's justification of this position it will be well to recall once again the distinction between (1) Categories, which are *a priori* notions applicable to manifolds of perception, and (2) Ideas, which are likewise *a priori* but not similarly applicable. In the case of the Categories, the method of showing the rightfulness of their use was by a Transcendental Deduction of them, i.e. by showing that a manifold of perception becomes an object of experience only through the application of the Categories to it. Any parallel treatment of an Idea is impossible for the obvious reason that it is not thus applicable; it does not refer to any manifold of perception and consequently does not confer upon any such manifold that objectivity which is characteristic of the objects of factual and scientific judgements.

Kant's justification for the assumption that man is morally free proceeds by two main steps. The *first* has already been taken. In the *Critique of Pure Reason* it has been shown that we can *think* man a *noumenon* outside the causal order of nature, and morally free. Moreover it has been shown that the two propositions 'Man as *noumenon* is free' and 'Man as *phenomenon* is part of the causal order of nature' are compatible. Indeed, Kant has argued that the Third Antinomy of Pure Reason can only be resolved by admitting the joint possibility of both these propositions, thereby accepting the position of transcendental idealism, that whatever stands under the forms of space and time and under the Categories 'is empirically real and transcendentally ideal'.

Within the field of mathematics and natural science – that is to say, within the field of the critique of pure reason – the concept of freedom has no positive content. There, freedom means nothing beyond independence of the causal order of nature. If we keep this in mind we can regard it as a kind of causality and contrast it, as moral or *noumenal*, with the positive notion of natural or phenomenal causality, which is a schematized Category of theoretical thinking.

We have established, now, the internal consistency of the notion of freedom or moral causality. But from the internal consistency of a notion we cannot infer that there are any actual instances of it whatsoever. From the internal consistency of 'centaur', for example, it does not follow that centaurs exist. No more can we infer from the internal consistency of the notion 'man as a *noumenon*' that man as a *noumenon exists*. If we wish to prove that man exists as a free being we need to know something more; and the nature of the additional evidence we require will determine in what sense we can attribute to man existence as a free being.

This additional evidence comes from moral experience. In appealing to it Kant is taking the *second* step of his proof that man is free. According to him, it is the plain outcome of ordinary moral experience that we apprehend the moral law and our subjection to it. This implies freedom. If the assumption (of our freedom) were self-contradictory there could be no such implication; our apprehension of the moral law would have to pass as an illusion and our moral judgements as mistakes. The assumption, however, we have found internally consistent: so our apprehension of the moral law can be evi-

dence of freedom. There is, moreover, no evidence against it.
To give the position in Kant's words:

'The moral law shows its reality, in a manner which is sufficient even from the point of view of the *critique* of theoretical
reason, in adding a positive characteristic to a causality which
so far has been conceived only negatively and the possibility
of which, although incomprehensible to theoretical reason,
had yet to be assumed by it. This positive characteristic is the
conception of reason as immediately determining the will
(through the condition that a universal form can be given to
its maxims as laws). Thus, for the first time, the moral law can
give objective (though only practical) reality to reason which
always hitherto had to transcend all possible experience when
it put its Ideas to a theoretical use . . .'[1]

Thus, the categorical imperative implies *that* we are free;
while on the other hand the assumption that we are so is
(a) internally consistent and (b) compatible with the principle
– a fundamental principle of the *Critique of Pure Reason* – that
all events are causally necessary. Thus we are justified in taking
our apprehension of the moral law as being what it seems to be
to our ordinary moral conscience – an absolute command
which *we can fulfil* in spite of our being part of the causal order
of nature. All this, however, does not mean that we can know
our moral freedom and its working in the same way as we
know instances of natural causality. There is, as Kant himself
insists, nothing in his argument, or indeed in his whole moral
philosophy, to alter the thesis that moral freedom is an Idea
of pure reason, and therefore unknowable. For the knowable
must be both thinkable *and* perceivable; while 'a perceivable
instance of an Idea' is, and remains, a logical contradiction.

If all our thinking were scientific or if it belonged to the
region of that commonsense reflection which is rudimentary
science, then it would make no difference whether we were
naïve realists or transcendental idealists. It makes an important difference if our thinking includes reflection not only upon
matters of fact but also on moral obligation. This is because we

1. *Pr. R.* 48, *Ab.* 137.

cannot in that case avoid being confronted with the *prima facie* conflict between the causal necessity of our actions as parts of the order of nature and our moral responsibility for them as free agents. If we cannot reject, as being mere mistakes, *either* our apprehension of natural necessity *or* our consciousness of moral freedom then we have no alternative but to treat Kant's theory with respect as one of the few thorough attempts to do equal justice to both science and morals.

Certainly the statistical conception of natural law does nothing to reconcile the two standpoints. It is sometimes said that since all laws of nature are merely statistical, science and morality can no longer conflict. It might be argued in support of such a view that if it were a *statistical* law that a certain percentage of action must always be done in violation of duty, then the law would leave room for the freedom of the will, since being merely statistical it would refer not to any particular action but merely to a certain proportion of actions. The argument, however, implies that a law of nature would rule out the possibility that all men should be able to do their duty simultaneously and continuously. Our subjection to the moral law, however, implies precisely this. The conflict between causal necessity and moral freedom remains unresolved.

Another, and very frequent though no more successful, attempt to solve the problem is found not only in philosophical books but also in the criminal codes of civilized countries. It consists in distinguishing between causes identifiable with the doer and causes which are outside his control. The doer may or may not be responsible. He is responsible according to the theory if he is or 'contains' the cause of his action, which is then, as it is put, 'freely chosen'. But if we accept the principle of natural causality, every event in time is caused and every cause is part of a causal chain which started before the birth of the doer. By receiving the title of 'freely chosen' a cause does not cease to have been caused. This way of tackling the problem, e.g., by calling inner causes 'free' and external causes 'mechanical', is no more than a way of ignoring it.

Kant calls it a 'miserable makeshift' and 'petty verbal hair-splitting'.[1]

We usually regard a person as responsible for his action *if he could have chosen* not to perform it. As G. E. Moore has pointed out, the sense of the phrase 'if he could have chosen otherwise' is difficult to determine. Indeed, however we take it, we seem to leave the doer either always or never responsible. On the one hand, the mere logical possibility of another action, i.e. its non-contradictoriness, is not sufficient since it is *always* logically possible to assume that an event fell out otherwise than in fact it did. On the other hand to require factual possibility (that a person, in order to be responsible, must have been able to change the course of the causal sequences leading to his action) is to require too much: for a person is never in this position and so would *never* be responsible for his action. To say that the possibility expressed by the phrase 'could have chosen' is neither logical nor causal, but *sui generis*, is, unless qualified by further suggestions, of little use.

Kant's answer, which follows from his distinction between man as a *phenomenon* and man as *noumenon*, is that it is incompatible with the principle of causality for any causal sequence to be changed. We cannot choose that an action be not the effect of its causes. But he also holds that man *as a noumenon* could have chosen differently since 'the whole chain of appearances with respect to anything which concerns the moral law depends on the spontaneity of the subject as a thing in itself. Of the nature of this spontaneity, however, a physical explanation is impossible.'[2]

For Kant the key to the understanding of the phrase 'if he could have chosen' is the subject of the choice, which is man as a *noumenon* or end in himself. The choice takes place on the noumenal level of human existence. We can infer, from an adequate description of theoretical and moral experience, *that* the choice takes place in the realm of *noumena*, but not *how* it does so. Indeed how it takes place is, like everything *noumenal* (non-phenomenal), unknowable.

1. *Pr. R.* 96, *Ab.* 189.   2. *Pr. R.* 99, *Ab.* 193.

Kant's solution of the conflict between causal necessity and moral freedom implies, as he admits, 'many difficulties' and 'is hardly capable of being clearly presented'. But, he rightly asks, 'is any other which has been or may be attempted, simpler and more easily understandable?'[1] The answer, I think, must be an emphatic no, unless we regard it as a solution of the problem to ignore either morality or science and refuse to consider them together.

To Kant's account of freedom it is often, and quite naturally, objected, that our own observable actions and choices are carried out in time whereas the 'actions' and 'choices' of the noumenal self are outside time and unobservable. The apparent mysteriousness of these notions seems to many too high a price to be paid for the consistency of causal necessity with moral freedom. According to Kant, however, we are faced with the choice on the one hand of distrusting science, moral experience, or both; on the other hand of trusting them but accepting the fact that a crucial aspect of our being must remain unknowable to us.

In one way Kant's notion of a noumenal self and its choices is no more mysterious than, e.g., Hilbert's notion of infinity. Both are ideal, limiting concepts by means of which we establish the internal consistency of a system of propositions: in Kant's case the system of moral *and* scientific propositions, in Hilbert's case the system of classical mathematics. Yet Kant's notions of the noumenal self and its choices are considered by him to demarcate the field of the knowable from an unknowable region beyond it; whereas Hilbert's notion of infinity is conceived as a highly ingenious and highly subtle technicality.

Kant's thesis of 'the whole chain of appearances with respect to anything which concerns the moral law' being chosen by the unknowable noumenal self operating outside time, is not without other parallels. It reminds us, for example, of the Platonic myth of Er according to which the soul after death 'must choose a [new] life which she will have to realize of necessity'.[2] It also reminds us of various religious doctrines

1. *Pr. R.* 103, *Ab.* 197.   2. *Republic*, x, 617E.

within and outside the European tradition. It would, however, be quite contrary to Kant's conception of philosophy and to his manner of inquiry to support his conclusions by making use of either myth or the appeal to any special religious experience or authority.

The scientist *qua* scientist assumes that every event stands under causal or, at least, statistical laws. The judge, and indeed everybody who makes decisions and who is capable of feeling guilt and remorse, assumes that men are morally responsible and therefore free. It is the task of the philosopher to render the relation between science and morality intelligible. In undertaking this he must face problems different from those which are peculiar either to science or to moral reflection. He can, therefore, expect but little help from the pure scientists or the pure moralists and would, I think, be unwise if he ignored what Kant has to say on the way in which practical reason can provide answers to questions which theoretical reason cannot even properly ask.

2. Duty and Moral Goodness

In the first half of the present century philosophers on the whole have been concerned more with analysis and clarification than with building philosophical systems. The reason for the prevalence of analytical philosophy may lie on the one hand in the failure of the post-Kantian philosophers who paid no heed to the Transcendental Dialectic; on the other hand in the great number of problems which arose from new ways of thought in the natural sciences and mathematics and from the consequent employment of new types of conceptual apparatus, the utility of which was much greater than their logical transparence.

The general movement of philosophical attention towards the analysis of concepts and conceptual systems had its effect on moral philosophy, although the conceptual tools of moral thinking had, in comparison with those of science and mathematics, undergone very little change. In the hands of Moore, Prichard, Ross and many others the questions which received most attention were those questions of traditional ethics which were analytical. The main contemporary problems in ethics can, I believe, be formulated as follows: First, can moral concepts be defined in terms of empirical concepts? Secondly, is there one moral concept in terms of which, together with empirical concepts, all other moral concepts can be defined?

The first question is clearly the more fundamental: for if moral concepts can be defined in terms of empirical concepts, the second question does not arise. It is easy to misunderstand the meaning of the question by confusing empirical propositions about people's making of moral judgements with the content of these judgements. The proposition that a person judges an action to be morally right and that his doing so has certain psychological, sociological, or other causes, is, of course, empirical. The moral philosopher, however, asks whether the proposition that a certain action is morally right is itself empirical. The answer to *this* is by no means obvious, if only because so many acute philosophers disagree about it while agreeing on the main features of moral experience.

Kant's answer to the question whether moral concepts can be defined in terms of empirical ones should now be clear. According to him there can be no such definition since, while all empirical concepts refer to *phenomena*, which are subject to natural causality, the concept of duty implies moral freedom. As regards the second and less important question, whether there is one moral concept in terms of which, together with other not specifically moral concepts, every other moral concept can be defined, his answer is again quite clear. He holds that the notion of the categorical imperative is the fundamental concept of moral thinking.

The concepts of the morally good and the morally evil, in particular, must, he holds, be defined in terms of the moral law. If the notion of the good were logically *prior* to the conception of the moral law the former 'could only be the conception of something the existence of which promises pleasure

... Since, however, it is impossible to see *a priori* which presentation [*Vorstellung*] will be accompanied by pleasure ... we
should be entirely dependent on experience if we wish to
determine what is ... good and what evil.'[1]

If 'being pleasant', or indeed any other empirical property,
were meant by the term 'morally good', then all our general
moral judgements would be empirical generalizations, of which
we could only say that *so far* no exception had been found to
them. Now this is clearly not so. The empirical generalization
that all men die before reaching the age of a thousand years is
quite different from the moral judgement that cruel actions
committed for the sake of cruelty are morally wrong. General
moral judgements are not provisional in the sense in which
general empirical judgements are. If we define the morally
good as *that which we can will in conformity with the categorical
imperative*, then a judgement to the effect that, e.g., a certain
action is morally good is not provisional.

Moral philosophers who have based their theories on the
assumption that there must be *an object* the desire for which is
morally good, are (Kant holds) whether they like it or not,
committed to an empirical theory of ethics. It does not matter
whether they regarded happiness, perfection, moral feeling, or
the will of God as this object. In each of these cases 'their principle was always heteronomy and they could not avoid being
confronted by empirical conditions of a moral law; since their
object, as an immediate determination of the will, could be
called good or evil only according to its immediate relation to
feeling, which is always empirical'.[2]

Kant's arguments are directed against any moral theory
which attempts to define the moral law or duty in terms of good
objects. Some contemporary moral philosophers, e.g. Ross,
would agree with him on this point. They would, however,
object to Kant's attempt to define moral goodness in terms of
the moral law or duty, because they hold that the notions of
duty and of moral goodness are both fundamental and not
interdefinable. Kant did not find this or any similar view in the

1. *Pr. R.* 58, *Ab.* 149.   2. *Pr. R.* 64, *Ab.* 155.

writings of his predecessors, and so did not explicitly discuss it. That he would not have agreed with it is clear from his actual definition of moral goodness in terms of duty.

After the publication of Sir David Ross's book *The Right and the Good* the question of the interdefinability of 'duty' and 'moral goodness' came rather into the foreground of philosophical discussion. The reason for this preoccupation with a problem which seems to be of strangely small importance was probably largely the almost general consent of philosophers that G. E. Moore had shown once for all that moral judgements are non-empirical statements of specifically moral facts. This reassuring view is no longer generally held; and moral philosophers are again more concerned with the fundamental question of the logical status of moral concepts and judgements in general than with establishing neat logical relations between them.

An important reason for defining the notions of 'moral goodness' or 'duty' or both in terms of *desires for specific ends* arises from the assumption that only such desires can move us to action. The notion of a desire for a specific but unspecified end is, as I believe, hopelessly vague; it may cover almost everything from the desire to eat a particular piece of food to the desire for a wholly undefined state of perfection. Opponents of Kant's ethical theory often argue that since every action must have a specific desire for its motive and since an action for the sake of duty would not be prompted by a specific desire there can be no such action. This argument seems to me no more than an example of begging the question at issue by means of suitable definitions.

This argument is often justified by an appeal to a famous statement in the sixth book of the *Nicomachean Ethics*: 'Thought by itself', Aristotle says there, 'moves nothing, but only thought directed to an end and concerned with action.' This statement is clearly incompatible with Kant's view that apprehension of the moral law or, more precisely, apprehension of the conformity of our maxim in a particular instance to the moral law, may of itself move us to an action. In certain situations the apprehension of a maxim as conforming to the categorical imperative will, according to Kant, make us fulfil a promise in spite of many desires to the contrary and without our having any 'specific end' in mind.

If we wish to decide whether the Aristotelian or the Kantian thesis is correct, we have first of all to ask ourselves what kind of statement Aristotle is making. Our answer must, I believe, be that he is making an empirical, or more precisely, a psychological assertion, about how people make up their minds to act. He holds that we always act in accordance with certain desires and implies that a conflict between duty and desire can lead to a dutiful action only if duty itself is based on (or is definable in terms of) a specific desire.

Now Kant does not accept Aristotle's description of how we make up our minds to act. He accepts the conflict between duty (which is unlike desire) and desire as a fundamental fact of moral experience, the explanation of which is one of the tasks of moral philosophy. The issue between Kant and Aristotle is thus not one of ethical theory but concerns the *data* of ethical theory or the proper description of moral experience. It is a question we may properly decide for ourselves. In order to decide it we must reflect upon our own experience of obligation and moral conflict. If we come to the conclusion that we sometimes experience a conflict between duty and desire and yet do our duty, then we cannot accept the Aristotelian objection: it is a description which does not fit our experience.

Apprehension of the moral law and of our duty is, according to Kant, always accompanied by a peculiar emotion or moral feeling which he calls *Achtung für das Sittengesetz* (respect or reverence for the moral law). Since our apprehension of the moral law always implies our having this emotion or moral feeling we may be led to think that the occurrence of the feeling is the criterion of the morality of an action and the source of our formulating maxims corresponding to the moral law. This view is, however, diametrically opposed to Kant's ethical position. The moral feeling caused by the apprehension of the moral law does 'not serve as a means of judging actions or even as the ground of the moral law itself, but only as a motive to make it one's maxim'.[1]

As has been pointed out (e.g. by Paton in *The Categorical Imperative*) Kant's statement that reverence for the moral law is a motive for adopting it as one's principle of action may seem incompatible with his central thesis that the moral law determines the will immediately. I believe, however, as Professor Paton does, that this real or apparent incompatibility should not be taken too seriously. The notion of reverence for the moral law is after all introduced only for the sake of describing the manner in which the moral law determines the will. It is an element in the complex situations which we call 'awareness of our duty' or 'conflict between duty and desire', an element the presence of which in no way excludes the possibility of the moral law's determining our will directly. If a philosopher's statements seem to contradict one of his central theses then these statements must be interpreted and, if necessary, modified in the light of his main doctrine. This we can do easily by regarding reverence, which is different from all desires and inclinations, as the necessary effect of the apprehension of duty by a being who is not only rational but is also possessed of desires. Indeed Kant's description and account of reverence fully supports this interpretation.

3. The Postulates of Practical Reason

We have seen that according to Kant man's subjection to a self-imposed moral law, which he can choose to obey or to violate, implies the assumption that man is morally free. This assumption, which could not be made about the phenomenal world without contradiction and must refer to man as a *noumenon*, is one of the three so-called postulates of practical reason, the other two being the assumption of man's immortality and the assumption of the existence of God.

'These postulates are not theoretical dogmata, but *presup-*

1. *Pr. R.* 76, *Ab.* 169.

positions which have necessarily only practical import. They consequently do not extend speculative [= theoretical] knowledge, but give to the Ideas of practical reason *in general* objective reality (by their relation to the practical) . . .'[1] The postulates of practical reason state that the Ideas of God, freedom, and immortality have 'objects' – but not, of course, objects which can be given to perception. They are not objects in the sense of the *Critique of Pure Reason*, that is to say, manifolds of perception which have synthetic unity or which are instances of the schematized Categories. They are non-phenomenal 'objects' whose existence is guaranteed only by the apprehension of the moral law.

To state that substances *exist* (or substance exists) or that the Category of substance has an object, is to state, roughly speaking, that the application of the Category is involved in every objective empirical (in every 'is-the-case') judgement. To state that freedom, immortality, and God *exist*, is to say that our having duties implies that the notions have instances which, since they cannot be phenomenal, must be *noumenal* and therefore unknowable.

The authority of the postulates of practical reason is only delegated. It depends on the one hand on the kind of authority which we find in the moral law, especially in comparison with mathematics and scientific knowledge. It depends on the other hand on the kind of connexion which links the apprehension of the categorical imperative to the postulates. This connexion is most direct and close in the case of the postulate of freedom and most tenuous in the postulate of God's existence.

It is possible to select statements from Kant's ethical writings which *taken by themselves* point to a pragmatist ethic according to which the concepts of morals are useful fictions. On this view the command to the effect that we should act in accordance with the moral law is 'analysed' into the command that we should act *as if* there were an absolute moral law. If this wholly un-Kantian view were accepted then, of course, the

1. *Pr. R.* 132, *Ab.* 229.

postulates of practical reason, which rest solely on the moral law, would also be fictitious.

At the other extreme we might hold that our apprehension of the categorical imperative is more assured than our apprehension of anything else. On such a view we might attach at least as much 'weight' to the *practical* objectivity of the moral law and its implications or necessary conditions as we attach to the *theoretical* objectivity of science and mathematics. It is not impossible that a great deal depends here on the experience of different persons. The voice of duty may speak in varying degrees of loudness and clarity. In any case a comparison between practical and theoretical objectivity lacks any even moderately precise standard. Kant's view of the practical objectivity of the moral law and consequently of the postulates of practical reason is far removed from pragmatism.

We must now turn to the manner in which the postulates of practical reason are related to the moral law. They condition practical objectivity. In the case of freedom the argument is fairly clear. The postulate that man is morally free and therefore, if we accept Kant's distinction between *phenomena* and *noumena*, free as a *noumenon*, follows directly, as we have seen, from our subjection to the moral law. To deny that we are, in an unknowable manner, morally free, is to deny that we apprehend the categorical imperative as categorical.

The argument by which Kant seeks to establish the connexion between the categorical imperative and the postulate of man's immortality is, I think, very much less convincing. 'The complete adequacy of the will to the moral law is *holiness*, a perfection of which no rational being is capable at any moment of his existence. Since, however, it is required as practically necessary it can be found only in a *progressus* which continues *into infinity* . . . This infinite progress is, however, possible only if we assume an *infinitely* lasting existence of the same rational being (which is called the immortality of the soul.)'[1]

On this argument C. D. Broad[2] holds that Kant's premisses

1. *Pr. R.* 122, *Ab.* 218.
2. *Five Types of Ethical Theory*, London, 1944, p. 140.

are inconsistent with each other. According to the one premiss moral perfection is attainable while according to the other it is not; for attainable 'only after an unending time' is 'surely equivalent to saying that it is not attainable at all'. I do not think that this accusation of logical inconsistency is justified. Kant holds, in common with many mathematicians of our own time, that an infinite sequence can be regarded as completed in a sense which is quite compatible with its having no last member. The notion of a completely given infinite sequence is for Kant an Idea which is internally consistent but to which nothing in the phenomenal world can possibly correspond. It is theoretically empty. In other words the assumption of a completed totality as an Idea of pure reason is compatible with the assumption that the *phenomenal* world contains no *actually* infinite sequences, but at best sequences which continue without coming to an end.[1]

In Kant's argument for immortality, as in that for moral freedom, he tries to show that the theoretically empty Idea is given practical objectivity by being a condition of the moral law. However, the categorical imperative commands us to act in such a manner that we can will the maxim of our action to become a general law. It does not command the achievement of holiness or the 'complete adequacy of the will to the moral law'. It may be quite possible for us to do our duty and yet impossible for us to achieve holiness. Only if we are, over and above the categorical imperative, subject to a command to become holy does, according to Kant's argument, the notion of immortality have practical objectivity. The reason why Kant's argument in justification of the postulate of immortality carries little conviction is not a logical flaw, but, I think, the fact that we do not recognize the command to achieve holiness as a law which we can possibly choose to satisfy.

The Idea of God (this is Kant's teaching in the *Critique of Pure Reason*), has no theoretical objectivity. The thesis follows unmistakably from the position of transcendental idealism, and Kant has been at great pains to show that theoretical argu-

1. See Ch. v.

ments professing to prove the existence of God are all based on fallacious reasoning. By calling the thesis 'that God exists' a postulate of practical reason, Kant implies that the moral law gives it practical objectivity.

The ethical argument for God's existence makes use of the conception of the highest good which implies complete morality and 'the happiness which is commensurate with it'. As moral beings we must demand not only an ideal state of affairs in which all rational beings are holy but also one in which their state of mind is characterized by the amount and kind of happiness which they deserve. What ought to be must be possible, since every moral obligation implies the (moral or *noumenal*) freedom to realize it.

'We *ought* to endeavour to promote the highest good (which therefore must be possible). Therefore we must *postulate* the existence of a cause of the whole of nature, which is different from nature, and which contains the ground . . . of the exact proportionateness of happiness and morality.'[1] God, the Ideal of Pure Reason is, Kant shows, such a cause. In other words his argument is that the highest good is not realizable unless God exists. Since, as he himself insists,[2] the possibility of realizing the highest good implies the possibility of man's achieving holiness, the ethical argument for the existence of God is, at the very least, exposed to the same objections as the argument for the immortality of the soul. And in addition it presupposes that it is man's duty to attempt bringing about the highest good and that this he can do only with the help of God. But a person could without self-contradiction recognize the categorical imperative and yet believe that it is not his duty to try to bring about the highest good, since this duty would imply the existence of God which he denies. This does not mean that he would not consider it his duty to act *as if* it were possible to promote the highest good.

If we might attempt a reduction of Kant's arguments, as it were, to their bare logical bones, they could be put somewhat thus: (1) Man can do his duty only if he is free. (2) Man can

1. *Pr. R.* 125, *Ab.* 221.   2. *Pr. R.* 124, *Ab. loc. cit.*

achieve holiness only if he is immortal. (3) Man can promote the highest good only if God exists. Now man's moral freedom is a necessary condition of his power to achieve holiness, which in turn is a necessary condition of the highest good's being realized and, therefore, also of the existence of God. In other words the existence of God entails the possibility of holiness and thus the immortality of the soul. The possibility of holiness entails man's freedom.

However, man's freedom does not entail his power to achieve holiness and his power to achieve holiness does not entail the realizability of the highest good and of God's existence. The logical connexion is strongest between the categorical imperative and moral freedom; between the categorical imperative and the existence of God it is at its least direct. This, to judge from his own words, seems to have been Kant's own view.

The beliefs in God, in immortality, and freedom are not 'meaningless' although they do not derive their meaning from statements of scientific fact. Their meaning according to Kant consists in the ways in which they are linked to what he regards as the fundamental moral experience: the apprehension of the categorical imperative.

4. Morality and Religion

Kant's view on the relation between morality and religion is contained in the *Critiques* of theoretical and of practical reason. It is further expounded and applied in *Religion within the Limits of Pure Reason* (1793). Its four parts were originally intended for publication in a learned periodical, but the second part failed to obtain the necessary approval by the Berlin censor.

The first sentences of the preface to this work set its whole tone and determine its character. 'Morality', Kant states clearly and firmly, '. . . needs the idea neither of another being above man for man to recognize his duty, nor of another motive apart from the law for him to fulfil his duty . . . Morality thus needs religion in no way for morality's sake, but is by virtue of the pure practical reason self-sufficient.'[1]

As we have seen, apprehension of the moral law gives rise to an Idea which implies the adequate correlation of virtue and happiness. Yet 'this Idea arises from morality and is not the ground thereof; it is an end the conception of which already presupposes moral principles'.[2] To this position Kant is committed by the central theses of his moral philosophy, which is based on the will's autonomy – its subjection to the self-imposed categorical imperative. To base morals on the command of God would be to make ethics heteronomous, which Kant regards as the crucial mistake of the moral philosophers who preceded him.

The *Critique of Pure Reason* has made room for faith by demonstrating that the conception of a most perfect being, though theoretically empty, is yet not logically absurd or self-contradictory. The *Critique of Practical Reason* has conferred some practical content on this concept by showing how through the conception of the highest good it is linked to the notions of duty and the moral law. In this way the two *Critiques* have prepared the ground for an act of faith which is in harmony with the findings of the critical philosophy. It can in this sense be called a rational faith. According to Kant it is rational also in the sense that it satisfies 'an interest of pure reason', namely in the connexion between the realms of nature and of moral freedom. However difficult it may be to understand Kant's notion of rational faith, he leaves us in no doubt that it is different from the apprehension either of the moral law or of the world of empirical fact. It belongs to the sphere of religion.

Although 'morality leads unavoidably to religion' an act of faith is required to close the logical gap between morality and the Idea of God as a 'moral legislator outside man'.[3] Kant distinguishes clearly between the various religious creeds and religion which by an act of faith gives life to the Idea of God, whose theoretical and practical possibility has been demar-

1. *Rel.* 3.   2. *Rel.* 5.   3. *Rel.* 6.

H

cated by the critical philosophy. 'There is only *one* true religion; but there can be many varieties of religious creeds ... It is, therefore, more appropriate to say: this man is of the Jewish, Mohammedan, Christian religious creed, than: he is of this or that religion.'[1]

It may be of some interest to note that very much the same view had been expressed by Lessing in the dramatic poem *Nathan the Wise* (1779), a play set in the Palestine of the Crusades and of the conflict between Christians, Mohammedans, and Jews. It is clearly expressed in a parable told by Nathan in which the three religious creeds are compared with three rings left by a loving father to his three sons. He had possessed a most precious ring, the true religion, but at least two of those which he gave to his sons, and possibly all three, must be mere imitations.[2]

The apprehension of the moral law is independent of religion. Yet the religious person will interpret the moral law as the command of God. According to the Bible[3] to obey the voice of God is 'better than sacrifice; and to hearken than the fat of rams'. For Kant all external worship is idle. '*Everything that man, apart from a moral way of life, believes himself to be capable of doing to please God is mere religious delusion* (Religionswahn) *and spurious worship* (Afterdienst) *of God.*'[4] This is a corner-stone of Kant's philosophy of religion and Kant's life bears testimony to this conviction. His biographer and personal friend, R. B. Jachmann, tells us that Kant, although deeply religious, abstained from all external religious customs. In his later years he certainly did not worship in church. There is, as I believe, no reason to doubt Jachmann's words. They are, moreover, confirmed by L. E. Borowski, another personal friend.

Kant respected every religious creed, and especially Christianity, for the moral doctrine which it contained. 'I distinguish', he says in a letter to Lavater (28.4.1775), 'the *teaching* of Christ from the *report* which we have of the teaching of Christ, and in order to get at the former I try above all to extract the

1. *Rel.* 108.   2. See act 3, scene 7.
3. I Samuel, ch. 15, v. 18.   4. *Rel.* 170.

moral teaching separated from all precepts of the New Testament. The former is surely the fundamental doctrine of the Gospel, the latter can only be an auxiliary doctrine . . .'

'I revere', he says in the same letter, 'the reports of the evangelists and apostles and put my humble confidence in that means of reconciliation of which they have given us historical tidings, or also in any other which God in his secret counsels may have hidden; for I do not in the least become a better man, if I can determine this means, since it concerns only that which God does; whereas I cannot be so bold and insolent to determine . . . this as the real means by which I expect my salvation . . . I am not near enough to the times from which they [the reports of the evangelists and apostles] have come to make such dangerous and arrogant decisions.'

There is nothing in Kant's published works on the philosophy of religion which is incompatible with the words or the spirit of this private letter. Kant believed, and believed he had demonstrated, that one can be truly religious without sharing the creed of any organized religion. He himself led the life of such a man.

5. The Relation of Kant's Ethics to some Contemporary Moral Theories

The two types of moral theory which, with many variants, are at the present time perhaps the most widely held in the English-speaking countries are on the one hand the view that moral concepts apply to a particular kind of fact; on the other hand the view that there is no such special realm of fact for their use, and that the terms are used for something else, for the expression and the evocation namely of attitudes. The most important representative of the former theory is G. E. Moore. One of the most lucid exponents of the latter is Professor C. L. Stevenson.

According to Moore, moral qualities – those we indicate by using moral terms – are not empirical or mathematical but are, as he puts it, 'non-naturalistic' qualities. Nevertheless, moral terms apply *in the first place* to facts and not, e.g., to attitudes or maxims. Moore's main argument in favour of this view[1] is based on the nature of moral disagreement which, he holds, is in every respect like disagreement about fact except that the moral concepts, the application of which is in question, are not empirical. Moral judgements are in particular regarded as objective in the sense that if they are true for one person and at one time they are necessarily true for any person and at any time.

Stevenson, on the other hand, holds that statements to the effect that something or other is morally good or right can be analysed by definitions whose general form he exemplifies as follows: '"This is good" has the same meaning as "This has qualities or relations X, Y, Z..." except that the word "good" has in addition a laudatory emotive meaning which permits it to express the speaker's approval and tend to evoke the approval of the hearer.'[2] To Moore's objection that if moral assertions merely served to express and evoke attitudes there could be no moral disagreement, Stevenson has his answer. It consists in pointing out that there are two kinds of real disagreement, namely those about facts and those in attitude. Thus, for example, the disagreement between parents about a child's education may be a mere disagreement in attitude. In his opinion moral disagreement can be well accounted for as disagreement in attitude.

Moore believes with Kant that moral judgements are not only objective but absolutely objective in a sense which excludes the possibility of alternative moral codes. Yet unlike Kant Moore offers no test for the morality of actions, either positive or negative, since he defines 'rightness' in terms of 'goodness' and holds the latter to be indefinable. In spite of the admirable clarity of its details Moore's moral theory leads to a result which may well seem – and does seem to me – obscure: to make a moral judgement is to apply an *unanalysable*

1. See, e.g., *Ethics*, London, 1912, pp. 100 ff.
2. *Ethics and Language*, Yale U.P., 1944, p. 207.

concept. This in itself would not matter much since, as Moore points out, colour predicates are also unanalysable. Colour-predicates are, however, ostensively definable, i.e. exemplifiable by pointing to clear examples such as colour-charts. Moore's unanalysable concept is not exemplifiable in any similarly unambiguous manner.

All that Moore can say about the unanalysable notion 'morally good' is, on the one hand, that it is *not* naturalistic – in a rather vague sense of that term; and on the other hand, that if anything is good its goodness is necessitated by all the non-moral characteristics which it possesses. This, according to Moore, is a necessary connexion which is *not* logical and *not* causal; and what it *is* Moore does not pretend to know.[1] As against this Kant analyses the moral judgement. He analyses it in terms of the conformity of maxims to a formal principle. Without committing what Moore called the naturalistic fallacy by defining moral predicates in terms of empirical ones, Kant shows clearly that they are objective, i.e. that they are practically objective in a clearly explained sense.

Stevenson believes with Kant that there is a strict distinction between theoretical thinking and morality. For the Kantian dichotomy of theoretical and practical *reason* he substitutes the dichotomy of descriptive and emotive *meaning*. While terms which characterize empirical facts have the former sort of meaning, terms which express and evoke attitudes have the latter. Yet I believe this distinction to be altogether too crude to lead to an adequate account of moral – or shall one say, presumptively moral – judgements. Although Stevenson insists that emotive meaning may have many shades and varieties he does not seriously set about to distinguish the use of 'good' in statements such as: 'This cheese is good', 'This poem is good', 'This action is (morally) good'. If he did I believe he would have to speak of maxims and principles of action rather than of the mere expression and evocation of attitudes. He would, I think, come much closer to the Kantian position.

It would be a mistake to believe that we have to choose

1. See *Philosophical Studies*, p. 275.

between Moore and Stevenson or even, more generally, between an ethical theory which implies absolute, objective moral judgements and one which makes morality a matter of taste and emotion. In the preceding chapter I have briefly argued that Kant's formal test does not establish the absolute morality of any given code of maxims but only whether it is a moral or an a-moral code. Just as in view of modern developments the *Critique of Pure Reason* must be modified to admit the possibility of scientific theories other than the Newtonian which Kant had accepted; so, I believe, must the *Critique of Practical Reason* be modified to accommodate moral systems other than that from which Kant draws his examples. It is a fallacy to think that by merely replacing, in both the theoretical sphere and in the practical, Kant's absolute objectivity by a relative one, either science or morality would *ipso facto* become matters of taste. In particular, it is fallacious to think that the categorical imperative would, by being recognized as only a negative test, become hypothetical.

This digression into contemporary ethical controversy must necessarily be sketchy and inadequate, but its purpose is merely to show, once more, the contemporary relevance of Kant's theory. It is certainly not intended as an exhortation to the reader to close his Moore and Stevenson, but rather as a recommendation to him to open, or reopen as the case may be, Kant's ethical writings.

CHAPTER EIGHT

KANT'S THEORY OF AESTHETIC TASTE

1. The Place of the Third Critique and the Principle of Reflective Judgement

THE Critiques of theoretical and of practical reason are a systematic survey of the *a priori* principles of empirical knowledge and of morality. They are not the whole system and not even the whole outline of the critical philosophy. The stage is not yet set for a mere filling in of details and 'for men of impartiality, insight and the real gift of popular explanation to devote themselves to giving it true elegance'.[1] Another *Critique* had to be thought out and written by Kant before, at the age of sixty-six years, he felt himself justified in stating[2] that he had 'concluded his whole critical business' and that he could now without delay proceed to the 'doctrinal' – the cultivation of those regions of which, as he believed, the critical philosophy had rightfully taken possession. This third *Critique* is the *Critique of Judgement*, 'Judgement' (in this sense here always spelt with a capital) meaning the power or faculty of judging (*Urteilskraft*).

In order to show the relation between the tasks of the three *Critiques* Kant uses the now obsolete and suspect language of faculties. Contemporary philosophers are, rightly, so I believe, no longer interested in assigning principles to certain faculties but in finding how these principles function in our actual thinking and conduct. It would, however, be a mistake to believe that Kant's main interest does not lie in the same direction. When he speaks of faculties it is his habit to look back or forward to an examination of function. This we have seen to be so in the first two *Critiques* and we can also expect it in the third.

1. *Pu. R.* 26, *B* XLIV.   2. *Ju.* 170.

In common with his rationalist predecessors Kant distinguishes between three faculties of the mind as a whole: (1) cognition, (2) the feeling of pleasure and displeasure (*Lust und Unlust*) and (3) desire. He also distinguishes between three cognitive faculties, namely (1) the Understanding, (2) Judgement, and (3) Reason. The *Critique of Pure Reason* has, he holds, uncovered the *a priori* principles of the understanding and shown that and how they legislate for empirical knowledge. The *Critique of Practical Reason* has similarly uncovered an *a priori* principle of Reason and shown that and how it legislates for desire. So far Judgement has not been assigned any *a priori* principles, and feeling, or judgements about it, has not been systematically examined.

'Judgement in general' is according to Kant[1] 'the faculty of thinking the particular as being contained in the universal. If the universal (the rule, the principle, the law) is given, then Judgement which subsumes the particular under it is *determinant*. If, however, the particular is given, to which Judgement is to find the universal, then it is merely reflective.' There is no problem about the *a priori* given principles of determinant Judgement. They are no other than the principles of the Transcendental Analytic, the application of which had been made clear in the doctrine of the transcendental schematism.[2]

If reflective Judgement has its *a priori* principles one of their functions would have to be to guide the search for general laws which are not given – *a priori* or *a posteriori*. Consideration of the system of faculties of the mind as a whole and of their corresponding cognitive faculties leads Kant to the conjecture that reflective Judgement has an *a priori* principle related to feeling in a way analogous to that in which the *a priori* principles of the understanding are related to knowledge of empirical fact and those of practical reason to desire. To prove this conjecture is one of the tasks of the third *Critique*.

Another task which still remains to be performed is to inquire into the connexion between the realm of nature and

1. *Ju.* 179.   2. See ch. IV, § 1.

that of moral freedom – between theoretical and practical reason. The first *Critique* has tried to show that the experience of empirical fact presupposes the adoption of certain synthetic *a priori* principles which together determine a conception of nature as a mechanistic system. The second *Critique* has tried to show that if moral action is not an illusion it is possible only if we assume a system of relative *and absolute* ends and our freedom to choose between their realization if they conflict with each other. The two *Critiques* are developed in the light of each other and by means of constant cross-reference. Together they show that the theoretically necessary principles, which apply to *phenomena*, and the practically necessary principles, which refer to *noumena*, are logically compatible.

Yet mere logical compatibility between the two sets of principles cannot be enough. There must be *some connexion* between the realms of freedom and of natural necessity: for our freedom finds realization in nature through our actions. 'There must, therefore, be a ground of this unity of the supersensible [the noumenal] which lies at the basis of nature with that which the notion of freedom contains as practically real.' The conception of this ground must moreover be such that 'it makes possible the transition from the way of thinking which is in accordance with the principles of nature to that which is in accordance with those of freedom'.[1] In the third *Critique* Kant sets out to show that reflective Judgement has an *a priori* principle which, among other things, also establishes the required harmony between nature and freedom.

It is clear that if there is such a principle it would have to be synthetic – its denial logically possible. It is indeed possible to deny without self-contradiction that beyond being mutually compatible the principles of natural science and morality are in any way linked together. Such a view would show great similarity to the doctrine of Averroes, Siger of Brabant, and other medieval philosophers that philosophical and theological truth, though compatible with each other, are wholly separate. The principle would, moreover, like the necessary principles

1. *Ju.* 176.

which it connects, have to be *a priori*, i.e. logically independent of any proposition which describes sense-impressions.

Reflective Judgement, the faculty of looking for the universal when the particular is given, is exercised in many fields of intellectual endeavour. It is by a consideration of its function in science that Kant sets about looking for its *a priori* principle. Science aims at discovering general laws in their systematic connexion. These laws are either synthetic *a priori* conditions of scientific knowledge, which conditions Kant believes to be discoverable, and to have been discovered (in the *Critique of Pure Reason*), or else they are empirical laws, i.e. *a posteriori* propositions, which can be discovered only by means of experiment and observation.

It is quite conceivable that the empirical generalizations which have been discovered or which await discovery by science constitute only an aggregate of isolated propositions or of isolated clusters of such, without any systematic interconnexion. An example of such an aggregate would be, let us say, a sociological theory which contained the following isolated generalizations and an indefinite number of others similarly detached each from all the rest: 'The increase in suicides in a given population is directly proportional to the number of its literate members', 'The increase in the number of death sentences in a given population is directly proportional to the increase in the number of its unemployed', etc. Generalizations cannot be simply swept into a heap and the result called a science. Whatever we precisely mean by a *system* of propositions, it is more than their mere conjunction.

The systematic unity of the *a priori* principles of science has according to Kant its 'ground in our understanding'. The unity of empirical principles, he therefore holds, can be no other than the assumption that 'the special empirical laws . . . must be *considered* . . . *as if* an understanding (though not ours) had given them for our faculties of cognition, in order to make possible a *system* of experience in accordance with special [empirical] laws of nature'.[1]

1. *Ju.* 180, my italics.

This assumption does not mean, as Kant insists and indicates by the use of 'as if', that the systematic unity of science presupposes the existence of God. It does mean that if science is to be possible the human understanding must be regarded as capable of apprehending the laws of nature, and that if God has created the world he has created an understandable world. Its import is similar to that of Einstein's aphorism, inscribed on a wall of the Princeton Institute for Advanced Study, that 'God is sophisticated but not malicious'.

The principle of the harmony between nature and our mental capacities is not itself legislative, but rather 'a principle of looking for laws, although a merely subjective one ...'[1] It is neither *theoretically* necessary as a condition of the experience of empirical fact being possible to us; nor *practically* necessary as a condition of 'duty' not being an empty notion. Its necessity is that of a heuristic principle the adoption of which is involved in the procedure not of this or that particular scientific undertaking, but of any scientific undertaking whatsoever. It embodies the fundamental and indispensable *As-If* of any search for a scientific system.

Kant's justification of the principle that nature is fitted to our purpose when we set out to discover the system of her laws reminds us of current justifications of induction. Reichenbach,[2] and many others after him, seek to justify induction by showing it to be a reasonable policy. Nature, they argue, either does or does not conform to discoverable inductive generalizations. If it does not then our empirical generalizations must be futile; if it does there is a chance of success. It is, therefore, a reasonable policy to make inductions.

The reasonableness of using inductive reasoning implies, of course, the reasonableness of the assumption that nature is fitted to our capacities of understanding; and to justify the former is *a fortiori* to justify the latter. However, even if for some reason or other we do not adopt induction as a policy of research we are still committed to assuming the principle of

1. *Ju.* 177.
2. *Wahrscheinlichkeitslehre*, Leiden, 1935, § 80.

reflective Judgement: for by rejecting it we imply the futility of any search for a system of empirical laws.

2. Reflective Judgement, Aesthetic Taste, Teleological Explanation

The requirement that nature be adapted to our purpose of understanding her implies, according to Kant, the further requirement 'that nature specify its general laws in conformity with a principle of purposiveness for our cognitive faculty, that is to say a principle of adaptation to the human understanding in its necessary function. It consists in finding for the particular which is presented in perception the universal; and in finding for different such universals [*zum Verschiedenen*] ... connexion in a unity of principle ...'[1] In employing reflective Judgement we demand purposive organization and proceed *as if* nature and its contents were so organized.

Just as the *Critique of Practical Reason* is not, *pace* Heine, the work of a repentant mechanist who wishes to find a place for objective morals and God; so the *Critique of Judgement* is *not* the expression of a nostalgic longing for the older ways of thinking in terms of final causes. The third *Critique* as a whole maintains in its integrity the mechanistic conception of nature as expounded in the *Critique of Pure Reason*. It examines only the function of the concepts of purposiveness, purpose, and final cause, and their relevance to aesthetic and scientific judgements.

One of the explanations of a natural event or process consists, according to Aristotle and his medieval followers, in indicating its purpose. This notion is used both in the sense of 'human purpose' and in a metaphysical sense in which it is not definable in terms of human desires. In the *Physics* (194b) Aristotle considers the example of a man who is taking exercise. If we ask *why* he takes exercise, the answer that he does so for the purpose of his health does satisfy us. The notion of

1. *Ju.* 186.

purpose in this context is quite clear. Its elements are (1) a desire for a state of affairs, health, (2) a purposive activity, the taking of exercise, and (3) the adaptedness of the activity to the purpose. It is, moreover, quite proper to regard the purpose as being in some sense prior to the purposive activity.

Aristotle, however, also holds that 'there is purpose . . . in what is and in what happens in Nature'. (199a.) He rejects the view that it is a mere coincidence 'that the front teeth come up with an edge, suited to dividing the food, and the back ones flat and good for grinding it, without there being any design in the matter'. He is aware of the objection which had been raised by Greek forerunners of Darwin, that 'in cases where coincidence brought about such a combination as might have been brought about by purpose, the creatures . . . having been suitably formed by the operation of chance, survived; otherwise they perished and still perish . . .'[1] In rejecting this view Aristotle uses a metaphysical notion of purpose or final cause which involves as its elements a purposive whole, and a purpose achieved by it, but no human desires. The sense in which the purpose here precedes the whole is difficult to grasp. It is at most analogous to the precedence of a human purpose to the purposive activity which fulfils it.

Kant in the *Critique of Judgement* is mainly concerned with the metaphysical notion of purpose, which is not dependent on human desires. He clearly distinguishes between the purposiveness of a particular whole and the purpose which it serves. He holds, moreover, that to the distinction between a purposive whole and its purpose there may correspond a real separation. The thesis[2] that 'Purposiveness can be without purpose' is most important for his theory of aesthetic taste. It is, as I believe, not at all a desperate or artificial assumption but an appropriate description of certain experiences. We often find particulars, whether man-made or not, whose parts are so intimately interrelated and so harmoniously fitted together and to the whole of which they are parts, that we speak of the whole as having a *design* without relating it either to a designer or to

1. P. 198b, Loeb translation.   2. *Ju.* 220.

a purpose for which it is designed. Indeed it often does not even occur to us to look for either. In a similar manner we can conceive of a purpose without being able to exhibit any organized whole serving it.

The distinction between purposive whole and purpose, in a teleological judgement, corresponds to the distinction between particular and concept in an ordinary (non-teleological) empirical judgement. The transition from one to the other is often, and quite naturally, made. Consider, for example, the empirical judgement 'This is a cat' which is easily transformed into 'This purposive whole serves the purpose of being a cat', or, in somewhat technical language, 'This purposive whole has as its final cause a cat's having to be'. In this transformation the particular has become a purposive whole, the concept 'cat' a final cause ('cat, *qua* final cause') and the copula 'is' has been replaced by the relation between a purposive whole and its purpose.

Since there can be purposive wholes without purposes and purposes to which no purposive wholes correspond, it is possible to examine them separately. Such a separation might even have great advantages, as we have seen in the first *Critique*, in which the *Transcendental Aesthetic* was concerned with particulars and the *Transcendental Logic* with general notions. A similar division is found in the *Critique of Judgement*. Its first part, the *Critique of Aesthetic Judgement*, is concerned with purposive wholes which are without specific purposes; such as, in other words, cannot be or are not subsumed under any definite final cause, not, that is, under any concept considered as final cause. Its second part, the *Critique of Teleological Judgement*, is mainly concerned with an examination of purposes or final causes without any specific purposive wholes which serve them.

The unity of the two parts follows from the principle of reflective Judgement, which demands the fittedness of nature to the purpose of our understanding. It leads us to make teleological judgements, it expresses our awareness of purposive wholes and our urge towards teleological explanation.

3. Judgements about the Beautiful

A judgement of aesthetic taste may either express a mere liking (or a dislike) or else it may in addition claim universal validity. In stating that I like, say, a picture or that it *seems* beautiful to me, I am not implying that another person to whom the picture does not seem beautiful is therefore mistaken. If, however, I state that the picture *is* beautiful, I am, at least apparently, claiming that anybody who judges it differently is in some sense wrong. The transition from a statement of private liking to one claiming universal validity reminds us of analogous transitions on the one hand from a merely perceptual to the corresponding objective empirical judgement (e.g. from 'This seems a heavy stone to me' to 'This is a heavy stone'); on the other hand from a statement of desire to one of duty (e.g. from 'Telling the truth is desired (or desirable)' to 'Telling the truth is a duty').

Can the claim of some aesthetic judgements to universal validity be justified? One point about the answer is clear already. The claim, and therefore its justification, is quite different from that of theoretically and that of practically objective (necessary, universal) judgements. That, if anything, which confers universal validity on a judgement of private taste, thereby changing it into a judgement about the beautiful – an 'is-beautiful' judgement – is neither the application of Categories nor the successful test by the formal principle of morality. The nature and justification of the claim to aesthetic objectivity can be discovered only by a careful examination of the whole class of judgements which implicitly make that claim.

Kant, as is his habit, conducts his examination on the lines of his formal scheme of the four classes of logical forms of judgement, namely quality, quantity, relation, and modality. This may seem strange if we consider that the application of Categories does not enter into judgements of taste. As we shall see, however, such judgements on Kant's view 'always involve a relation to the understanding'.[1] To each of the four classes of logical forms there corresponds a partial definition of what is meant by asserting that an object is beautiful. Although the arrangement of the partial definitions is, so I believe, artificial the definitions themselves are highly illuminating.

Perhaps the most important of these partial definitions is given under the heading of 'relation'. There, beauty is defined 'as the form of purposiveness in an object in so far as it is perceived *apart from the presentation of a purpose*'.[2] By distinguishing between the form and the matter of purposive wholes Kant implies that the form is given to all percipients while the matter is private to each. He moreover implies that judgement about objects' being beautiful concerns the shareable or public features of aesthetic experience.

The same purposive whole can become the subject both of a teleological judgement and of a judgement of aesthetic taste. When observing, say, a graceful galloping horse we may admire the harmonious interplay of its parts as serving a specific purpose such as the self-preservation of the animal. This type of admiration would be expressed by a teleological judgement. We may, however, admire the same harmonious whole apart from any purpose which it serves and even apart from any concept (e.g. 'horse' or 'running horse') which it exemplifies. Our admiration would then be purely aesthetic and expressed by a purely aesthetic judgement. We might say either that this object, which is in some way or other identified, is beautiful; or that this horse is beautiful. In the latter case we should use 'horse' only as a means of identifying the purposive whole which we are judging.

There are 'purposive' wholes which cannot, without being mis-described, be referred to any determinate purpose or subsumed under any determinate concept. The harmonious interplay and interdependence of sounds in a musical composition or of colours in a landscape are cases in point. Indeed the art of many modern painters, and of non-representational artists

1. *Ju.* 203, footnote. 2. *Ju.* 236.

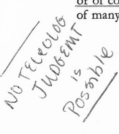

NO TELEOLOG JUDGEMT is Possible

in general, seems to be directed to the creation of 'purposive' wholes which cannot, even by the most insensitive public, be referred to any purpose or any determinate concept.

Kant's notion of purposive wholes which have no purpose may seem deliberately paradoxical and perverse. Yet he has at least two very good reasons for employing it. On the one hand the notion draws attention to the similarity between a beautiful object and an organism both of which exhibit a complex interdependence of their parts; while at the same time drawing attention to the difference between them which lies in the fact that the organism but not the beautiful object is referred to a specific purpose. On the other hand the notion of purposiveness implies the active imposition of an order on what otherwise would be a mere manifold of perception.

The imposition of order and unity on a manifold of perception is, according to one of Kant's fundamental assumptions, the work of the understanding. Its logical mechanism in conferring objectivity on empirical judgements has been explained in the *Critique of Pure Reason*.[1] There he distinguishes between (1) the given manifold of presentations, (2) their collection by the imagination, (3) the application of a Category which confers objective empirical reference. The unity of an aesthetic, purposive whole does *not* involve the third feature. What is collected by the imagination has unity. It is a unity consisting in the reference to 'indeterminate concepts'; it is conferred on what has been collected by the imagination through the understanding but not through determinate or specific concepts. The aesthetic judgement concerns in Kant's words 'merely the relationship of the representative powers [the imagination and the understanding] in so far as they are determined by a presentation'.[2] Aesthetic experience does not involve the application of concepts but is 'the consciousness of the merely formal purposiveness in the interplay of the cognitive faculties of the subject on the occasion of a presentation . . .'[3]

Kant's first partial definition of beauty in terms of purposiveness without purpose finds a natural place in his philosophical

1. See ch. III, § 3 above.   2. *Ju.* 221.   3. *Ju.* 222.

system and expresses what many creative artists have expressed in less technical, and therefore perhaps more ambiguous, terms when trying to describe works of art. I cannot do better than quote Mr E. M. Forster. Speaking about *Macbeth*,[1] he says, ' Well, the play has several aspects – it is educational, it teaches us something about legendary Scotland, something about Jacobean England and a good deal about human nature and its perils. We can study its origins, and study and enjoy its dramatic technique and the music of its diction. All that is true. But *Macbeth* is furthermore a world of its own, created by Shakespeare and existing in virtue of its own poetry. It is in this aspect *Macbeth* for *Macbeth*'s sake, and that is what I intend by the phrase "art for art's sake". A work of art – whatever else it may be – is a self-contained entity, with a life of its own imposed on it by its own creator. It has internal order. It may have external form. That is how we recognize it.'

It will be well, perhaps, here to say a little more about the connexion between the interplay of imagination and understanding, and the 'purposeless purposiveness' of beauty. The latter notion can be understood independently of Kant's philosophy, since it is characteristic of many recognizable and familiar experiences of aesthetic awareness. The notion of the interplay of imagination and understanding in so far as it is an interplay *determined by a presentation without the mediation of concepts*, can be little but an empty abstraction for anybody not acquainted with the main argument of the first *Critique*. Its chief function is not so much to be a description of aesthetic experience as to relate aesthetic to other types of experience, in particular to that type which can be formulated in an objective empirical judgement. In this connexion we must never forget that on Kant's view the understanding suggests order. Understanding is the process of bringing order and unity into any manifold of perception, and on the other side imagination is not capricious, like fantasy or fancy or however we name the process by which we might combine, e.g., the likeness of a horse and of a man into the picture of a centaur.

1. *Two Cheers for Democracy*, London, 1951, p. 99.

A second partial definition of beauty is given under the heading of 'modality': 'Beautiful is that which, without a concept, is recognized as the object of a necessary pleasure.'[1] In judging of anything that it is beautiful we 'assume agreement'[2] on the part of everybody who perceives it. This ascription (*ansinnen*) to everybody, of agreement, presupposes a sense common to all human beings 'which, however, is no external sense but merely the effect of the free interplay of our cognitive powers'.[3] By speaking of a *free* interplay of the imagination and the understanding Kant reminds us again that the unity of aesthetic experience, although brought about by the understanding, is not an application of concepts.

The necessary connexion is quite different from any other since it holds not between two judgements or concepts but between the purposive whole and the feeling of pleasure. It is based on the assumptions that not only the achievement of a specific purpose, but also the mere awareness of purposiveness, gives us pleasure; and that the cognitive powers of all human beings are constituted alike so far as the apprehension of aesthetic wholes is concerned.

According to the second partial definition of beauty, judgements to the effect that something is beautiful express attitudes which do not vary from person to person. They are rooted in a disposition common to all beings combining in their constitution the faculties of imagination and understanding. On such a view it may be difficult to account for aesthetic disagreements. But it is not impossible. We might, for example, explain a person's mistake about what is beautiful as a mistake in his reading of his own state, reporting himself perhaps aesthetically repelled by some beautiful object when, at some deeper level, so to speak, he appreciated it – or *vice versa*. That would be one way. Another would be to trace his mistake to his not having 'seen' the object properly, his failure to identify the purposive whole, as when one is confronted with some work of art, the structure of which discloses itself to us only after much attention,

1. *Ju.* 240.   2. *Ju.* 237.   3. *Ju.* 238.

labour, and patience. Many modern musical compositions or paintings might well illustrate this point.

The third partial definition of beauty, given under the heading of 'quality', characterizes the pleasure connected with the apprehension of a beautiful object as being 'without any interest whatsoever'.[1] By 'interest' Kant understands here the pleasure which we take in the *existence* of an object. In aesthetic experience we are not concerned with the existence, but with 'the mere presentation' of the object.[2] Indeed we might say that Kant's exclusion of specific concepts, which could conceivably have been applied to a beautiful whole, prevents the latter from becoming a part of objective experience, and thus existing as a matter of empirical fact and as an object of interest. The disinterestedness of aesthetic taste, however, is generally agreed upon and need not be laboured. It is certainly not peculiar to Kant's position.

The same applies to the last of Kant's partial definitions of beauty. This he gives under the heading of 'quantity'. According to it 'that is beautiful which, without a concept [i.e. without being subsumed under any concept], pleases universally'.[3] This definition, so I believe, is implied by the second of those given above. It is required by architectonic considerations the ultimate source of which is Kant's conviction that the Aristotelian classification of judgements according to quantity, quality, relation, and modality is fundamental not only to the Understanding and to Practical Reason, but also to reflective Judgement.

Kant distinguishes two kinds of beauty: 'free beauty' and 'merely adherent beauty',[4] the beauty being adherent if the beautiful object is referred to a specific purpose, free if it is not. By making this distinction Kant, as I understand him, allows for those aesthetic experiences in which we apprehend a purposive whole (a) as serving a specific purpose, but at the same time also (b) as apart from it. 'Flowers', he says,[5] 'are objects of free natural beauty' since, except as botanists, 'we

1. *Ju.* 211.   2. *Ju.* 205.   3. *Ju.* 219.
4. *Ju.* 229.   5. *Loc. cit.*

do not know what sort of thing a flower is.' While the layman can see a flower only as an instance of free beauty and not also as something serving a purpose, the botanist can apprehend the beauty of a flower both as free *and* as adherent. The distinction between free and adherent is thus not a classification of things but rather a distinction between two modes of apprehending 'purposive' wholes.

In giving this account of judgements about the beautiful Kant has implicitly given a justification of their claim to universality. In making them, reflective Judgement 'is directed to that subjectivity ... which can be assumed in all men ...'[1] This is the core of the 'Transcendental Deduction' of judgements of aesthetic taste.

4. Beauty, Sublimity, and Moral Experience

The author of an admirably lucid, and, for this reason alone, quite exceptional book on aesthetics which was first published in 1914, tells us that 'courage is wanted, though no longer example', to deny the existence of sublimity as something clearly distinguishable from beauty.[2] It would seem, however, that in view of the general decline of interest in aesthetics, courage is no longer needed for the expression of any particular aesthetic view. Perhaps it is needed by those who still profess an unfashionable concern with aesthetics at all, as a philosophical subject.

However this may be, the discussion about the differences between the sublime and the beautiful, which started with Longinus and excited the philosophers and poets of the eighteenth century, has run its course. The reason for its fading away from the philosophic scene is, so I believe, mainly the recognition that a neat dichotomy of aesthetic experiences into those of the beautiful and those of the sublime misrepresents their great variety and their affinities. Yet, even if a sharp dis-

1. *Ju.* 290.
2. E. F. Carritt, *The Theory of Beauty*, 1949, p. 220.

tinction – as was attempted by Kant and some of his contemporaries and predecessors – must be artificial, a rough distinction which admits of a large region of hybrids between
the beautiful and the sublime can be useful and illuminating.

Kant devotes a whole, and fairly long, chapter of the third
Critique to an account of sublimity. This 'Analytic of the
Sublime', as he calls it, he regards as the transcendental coun-
terpart to Burke's merely 'physiological' or psychological
treatment of sublimity.[1] In a similar manner he had compared
the first *Critique* with Locke's 'physiological' essay concerning
human understanding.

Before turning to Kant's account of the sublime it is well to
call two examples to mind which illustrate his distinction between beauty and sublimity. We might, to take Kant's own
illustration, think on the one hand of the experience which
we have in admiring, without reference to specific purposes or
concepts, a beautiful flower; on the other hand the awesome
and yet in some respects pleasant feeling which arises from the
contemplation of the stormy sea.

The main difference between the sublime and the beautiful
lies according to Kant in the following features. First, 'the
beautiful in nature relates to the form of an object which consists in limitation; the sublime on the contrary is also found in
a formless object in so far as *limitlessness* . . . is resented, to
which nevertheless the thought of totality is added. Thus the
beautiful can, as it were, be taken as the representation of an
indeterminate concept of the Understanding, the sublime as
the representation of an indeterminate Idea of Reason.'[2]

Secondly 'the most important and indeed the inner difference between the sublime and the beautiful is very likely this:
. . . natural beauty . . . carries with it a purposiveness in its
form, by which the object somehow seems to be predeter-
mined for our Judgement; whereas that which in us . . . gives
rise to the feeling of sublimity may in its form appear to oppose

1. *A Philosophical Inquiry into the Origin of Our Ideas of the Sublime
and the Beautiful*, 1756.
2. *Ju.* 245.

our Judgement [*zweckwidrig für unsere Urteilskraft*], to be inadequate to our power of representation – in a sense to do violence to our imagination. Yet in spite of this it is judged to be the more sublime.'[1]

The passages quoted contain an introspective description of two types of aesthetic experience which rarely occur in the pure form of Kant's examples. Their main importance is not so much description, as the connexion of the experience of limitlessness with the Ideas of Reason, which have their ground in the demand that unlimited sequences be thought as completed. The stormy sea in itself 'cannot be called sublime. The sight of it is horrible, and one must have filled one's mind with all manner of Ideas if by such perception it is to be attuned to a feeling which is itself sublime because by it the mind is incited to abandon the realm of sense and to concern itself with Ideas involving a higher purposiveness.'[2]

The traditional distinction between the beautiful and the sublime is incomparably vaguer than that between concepts and Ideas. By connecting the two distinctions, in referring the beautiful to indeterminate Concepts and the sublime to indeterminate Ideas, Kant has strengthened the systematic unity of the critical philosophy and enhanced its architectonic beauty. But this gain is achieved at the price of an over-simplified description of aesthetic experience. The term 'purposiveness without purpose' is wide enough to cover the peculiar unity and coherence of which we are aware in aesthetic experience, in an unlimited number of ways which admit of rough grouping rather than of precise classification.

Kant is not content with the sharp distinction between the beautiful and the sublime but goes on to distinguish between two kinds of sublimity: the mathematically and the dynamically sublime. The former is explained in terms of 'a movement of the mind' caused by an interplay of the imagination and cognition, the latter by an interplay of the imagination and desire – in both these cases 'without purpose or interest'.[3] The mathematically sublime is 'great beyond all comparison'.[4]

1. *Loc. cit.*   2. *Ju.* 246.   3. *Ju.* 247.   4. *Ju.* 248.

'Nature judged as power in an aesthetic judgement is dynamically sublime.'[1] In either case the sublime 'pleases immediately
by virtue of its opposition to the interest of the senses'.[2]

It is impossible here to follow Kant's argument in all its
ramifications. Its main outline, however, which I have tried to
indicate, shows that the third *Critique* is intimately related to
the other two. A reader who tried to study it in isolation would
be in great danger of mistaking many of its most significant
statements for empty abstractions, and of misunderstanding
many others. In the course of his account of aesthetic experience and aesthetic judgement Kant raises many issues which
are of general interest. I shall conclude this section by touch-
ing upon some of them.

A brief indication of his view of the relation between
aesthetic and moral experience could, apart from any other
reason, be amply justified as a demonstration that statements
about 'beauty and goodness' need not be trite or unctuous.
It is based mainly on a consideration of the ways in which
various types of general notion are related to sense-experience.
There is, of course, no problem about *a posteriori* notions.
They are exemplifiable in a straightforward manner.

The *a priori* concepts which have been dealt with in the
Transcendental Analytic of the first *Critique* cannot be exemplified. They can, however, be schematized. In other words
'the corresponding perception is given *a priori*'.[3] How this is
achieved has been explained at some length.[4] We have also
seen that the Ideas of Reason can neither be exemplified nor
schematized. They can, however, be indirectly represented by
means of analogies, that is to say they can be *symbolized*.

Kant gives an illuminating example of what he means by
symbolic representation. 'A monarchic state is symbolically
represented by an animated body if it is governed according
to laws which spring from the people [*nach inneren Volksgeset-
zen*]; but as a mere machine such as a handmill, if it is governed
by a single absolute will ...'[5] The representation is in both

1. *Ju.* 260.　　　2. *Ju.* 267.　　　3. *Ju.* 351.
4. Ch. IV, § 1 above.　　　5. *Ju.* 352.

these cases merely symbolic. It draws attention not to a similarity between a despotic state and a handmill but to one 'between the rules according to which we reflect upon both and their causality'.[1] Kant considers a deeper inquiry into the problem of symbolic representation important but not in place in the context. It is, so I believe, a philosophical task still outstanding.

Kant's view of the relation between aesthetic and moral experience is that the beautiful is a symbol of the morally good. There is in other words a similarity in the way in which we think about them, which is expressed even in ordinary language. We call beautiful objects of nature or art by names 'which seem to be based on moral judgement. We call buildings or trees majestic ... even colours are called innocent, modest, tender, because they arouse sensations which contain something analogous to the consciousness of a state of mind caused by moral judgements.'[2] The analogy between the morally good and the beautiful can be seen in many ways. Both are apprehended as immediately pleasing. The harmony between the free imagination and the order-imposing understanding corresponds to the conformity of the free will to its own legislation. There is an analogy between the claims to universality of aesthetic and moral judgements and between the ways in which the apprehension of the moral law gives rise to the emotion of respect and the apprehension of purposiveness gives rise to disinterested pleasure.

What Kant says about art and its relation to nature is to some extent coloured by his own taste. His favourite poets were Milton, Pope, and the didactic German poet Haller. He has little sympathy for romantic poetry and advises the romantic poet and thinker Herder to model his style on Pope and Montaigne. Kant had little feeling for music and his taste in painting would probably have precluded him from calling, say, Matisse a painter at all. His literary and artistic taste shows itself naturally more in the examples which he chooses to illustrate his theory than in the theory itself. Kant's lack of

1. *Ju.* 353.   2. *Ju.* 354.

perception for some works of art is no reason in itself for condemning his aesthetic theory. This would be as mistaken as the condemnation of *Gestalt* psychology on the ground that one of its exponents proved to be incapable of perceiving some types of *Gestalt*.

A work of art must according to Kant be recognizably art, as opposed to nature; yet 'the purposiveness in its form must appear to be as free from any compulsion of arbitrary rules as if it were a product of mere nature'.[1] This passage might be interpreted as implying the view that what would be disproportionate in nature would also be bad art and that nature provides strict standards of beauty in art. The view, however, that there are any conceptual standards or criteria of beauty either in art or in nature is quite incompatible with the spirit and even with the letter of Kant's philosophy of taste. Indeed 'the notion of fine art does not permit us to derive the judgement about the beauty of its product from any rule which has a concept as its ground . . .'[2] The apprehension of beauty does not involve the application of any specific concept.

Judgements of aesthetic taste seem to have two conflicting features: their being matters of taste and their claim to universality. We say with conviction that everybody has his own taste and that *de gustibus non est disputandum*. We claim, however, with equal conviction that the beauty of *King Lear* or the Moonlight Sonata should be recognized by everybody. Kant expresses this conflict as an antinomy – the 'antinomy of aesthetic Judgement'.

Its thesis asserts: 'A judgement of aesthetic taste is not based on concepts; if it were it would be a matter for dispute (for decision by means of proofs).' Its antithesis asserts: 'A judgement of taste is based on concepts; for otherwise there could not even be any disagreement about diverse judgements of taste (we could not even claim necessary agreement between that of others and our own).'[3] The root of this antinomy lies near the surface and is easier to diagnose than are the antinomies of *Pure Reason*, which require a subtle analysis

1. *Ju.* 306.   2. *Ju.* 307.   3. *Ju.* 338, 339.

of the notion of infinite totalities which are yet not completed.

The antinomy is resolved by showing that the contradiction between its thesis and its antithesis is only apparent. The thesis should be formulated more precisely as saying that a judgement of taste is not based on *determinate* or specific concepts. This follows from Kant's account of beauty as purposiveness without purpose, which is apprehended as the adaptiveness of presentations to the free interplay between the imagination and the understanding, i.e. as not involving the application of specific concepts. The antithesis should say that the judgement of taste is based on an *indeterminate* concept, which again implies that it does not involve the application of specific concepts. 'The antinomy which is here presented and resolved rests upon the correct notion of taste, namely as merely reflective Judgement. The two apparently incompatible principles can therefore be reconciled since *both may be true*; and this is sufficient.'[1]

1. *Ju.* 341.

CHAPTER NINE

TELEOLOGICAL EXPLANATION

1. The Subject of the Critique of Teleological Judgement

THE transference of general methodological assumptions which have proved useful in one field of inquiry to others seems reasonable policy even if its success or failure can rarely be predicted. Important historical examples of such transplantation are on the one hand the spread of teleological explanation which is typical of much medieval thought; on the other hand the spread of mechanistic explanation which characterizes the rise of natural science.

There can be little doubt that Aristotle's conception of explanation as being mainly teleological arose from his great interest in the phenomena of organic life and social organization and from the fact that he found this mode of interpreting them intellectually satisfying. For him and his medieval followers the understanding of nature was not as intimately linked with the power of making new things as it is for the modern scientist. They consequently could be content with teleological explanations in their thought not only about man but about any other subject matter including inorganic things and processes.

After the great success of the mechanistic principle in physics which culminated in the Newtonian system this new mode of thinking was with ever increasing frequency applied in other inquiries. Thus to give an outstanding example, Hobbes aimed at a science of man and society deliberately modelled on physics. Individual men are regarded for the purposes of this science as atoms, all alike in being selfish, and in being governed by the same psychological laws of motion. If we know the 'initial positions' of the atoms of any society, we can predict its future 'states'. This is one of Hobbes's central assumptions however he may have obscured it at times by other considerations. It is still with us in a great deal of psychological and economic thought. The greatest achievement of mechanistic explanation outside physics is Darwin's theory of natural selection and the evolution of species which centres in the mechanistic conception of the survival of the fittest, i.e. the survival of individuals and species in their environment.

Compared with the rapid progress of the physical sciences which was a direct result of the new non-Aristotelian ways of interpreting nature, the progress of the biological and in particular the social sciences has been slow. As a consequence of this the superiority of mechanistic over teleological explanation in these sciences has never been generally recognized by all the workers in these fields. No respectable physicist would dream of a teleological physics, however much his faith in the Newtonian system were shaken by recent developments. But the possibility of a teleological biology is by no means regarded as absurd and is at least thought worthy of refutation by biologists and philosophers.

Kant lived at a time when mechanistic explanation had already achieved its greatest triumphs in physics. In biology on the other hand and in the social sciences it was at best a scientific programme and certainly not a scientific reality. To Kant it seemed absurd to hope 'that one day there would arise a second Newton who would make intelligible the production of a single blade of grass in accordance with laws of nature the mutual relations of which were not arranged by some intention ... ' 'Such insight', he says, 'must be utterly denied to man.'[1]

Kant believed both that a scientific explanation must be mechanistic (Newtonian) and that biological phenomena – though in some respects open to it – do not admit completely of a mechanistic explanation. It therefore becomes an important task of the critical philosophy to examine the notion of

1. *Ju.* 400.

purpose and the manner of its legitimate and illegitimate employment in science. More particularly it becomes necessary to examine the relation between mechanism and teleology.

In our own day the situation with regard to the problem treated of in the *Critique of Teleological Judgement* has become more complex. Mechanistic explanation has in many cases, even in physics, been unsuccessful and other quite different types of non-teleological explanation have been successfully tried there. The issue is no longer simply between mechanistic and teleological explanation. Nevertheless while mechanistic explanations are sought and employed even now in every science, the nature and function of teleological judgements in the biological and social sciences is still under discussion. We have here another case in which Kant's examination of a philosophical problem has more than a merely historical interest.

In the widest sense of the term all judgements involving a notion of purposiveness or purpose are teleological. The differences between their various types are so great that it would not be profitable to try to deal with all of them at the same time. In the second part of the third *Critique* Kant is mainly concerned with a class of teleological judgements which can be fairly well distinguished from others by two characteristic features: (1) they are intended as explanations of the *existence* of things and (2) they are not explanations in terms of such human purposes and desires as vary from person to person. They are judgements about purposes in nature. Examples would be 'Small animals exist for the purpose of being eaten by larger ones' or 'The parts of any organism exist for the purposes of and by means of each other and of the whole to which they belong'.

Judgements about specific human purposes, say 'The Eskimos build igloos for the purpose of shelter', do not give rise to any new problems beyond those raised by judgements about desires. These have to some extent been discussed in the *Critique of Practical Reason*, which, among other things, is an account of the conflict between desire and duty. There it has been shown that an explanation in terms of human desires and purposes does not differ from any ordinary causal explanation.

There are, however, teleological judgements which are not meant to explain the existence of anything and are not even about existing things but merely about presentations. Aesthetic judgements, according to Kant, state a necessary connexion between 'the mere presentation of an object' as purposive and the pleasure accompanying it. This 'purposiveness', we remember, is apprehended apart from any determinate purpose. Indeed if it were related to a human purpose or a purpose in nature the experience would cease to be purely aesthetic. An aesthetic judgement, Kant insists, is based on that 'which in my mind I do with a presentation' and not 'on anything with respect to which I depend on the existence of the [presented] object'.[1]

Another type of teleological judgement is found in pure mathematics. For example, the theorem that the geometrical locus of all triangles with a given base and a vertical angle opposite it is a circle, is a *suitable ground* for the construction of any of these triangles. Kant regards this suitability as a purposive connexion – a 'purposiveness without purpose'.[2] In being independent of specific human desires it is similar to aesthetic purposiveness. It is, however, not the result of the harmonious interplay of the imagination and the understanding, which is necessarily accompanied by pleasure; but is a purely 'intellectual purposiveness' rooted in synthetic *a priori* principles and *a priori* constructions in space.

Teleological judgements about 'purposiveness' in mathematics differ from judgements about purposes in nature, in that they are *not* about existing things. 'Because pure mathematics does not deal with the existence, but only with the possibility of things – namely with pure perceptions corresponding to its [*a priori*] concepts – . . . all purposiveness found in mathematics must be regarded as merely formal.'[3]

In distinguishing between different types of teleological judgement Kant uses the over-worked terms 'formal' and

1. *Ju.* 205. 2. *Ju.* 364. 3. *Ju.* 366, footnote.

'material', 'subjective' and 'objective' in a special sense which
is not easily grasped and does not, so I believe, fully agree with
his own terminology in other parts of the critical philosophy.
These disagreements are of little consequence. Teleological
judgements are material if they refer to existing things; otherwise they are formal. Teleological judgements are, moreover,
subjective if they refer to the feelings or desires of the person
making them; otherwise they are objective.

He thus seems to have the following fourfold classification
in mind: (1) formal and subjective teleological judgements of
which aesthetic judgements are his only example; (2) formal
and objective teleological judgements of which judgements
about certain connexions in mathematics are his only example;
(3) material and subjective teleological judgements, i.e. judgements about human purposes; and lastly (4) material and objective teleological judgements, i.e. judgements about purposes
in nature. Whether or not this classification is as neat as he
believed, Kant makes it quite clear why he regards all aesthetic
judgements, some mathematical judgements, and all judgements about human and non-human purposes as teleological.
In the illuminating modern fashion of speaking, introduced by
Wittgenstein, we might say that by calling all the above-
mentioned types of judgement 'teleological' Kant has drawn
attention to important general family resemblances between
all of them and to even closer resemblances between those
which he classifies under the same heading.

2. The Notion of Purpose in Nature

According to the doctrine of the *Critique of Pure Reason* all
phenomena stand under the synthetic *a priori* principles of the
Understanding. Thus in particular every change happens to a
substance or substances and must have a cause. To give a
causal explanation is, schematically speaking, to state that an
event of type A involving certain things causes an event of
type B involving these or other things. Consider, to give a

very simple example, the sequence of events in which a weaker animal, such as an antelope, comes near a stronger carnivorous animal, such as a lion, and is subsequently killed and fed upon by the lion. A causal explanation of these events, if we can find one, would consist in showing that the two events belong to two distinct types and that an event of the first type leads with causal necessity to an event of the second type. The principle of causality does not, as Kant has made quite clear, in any way guarantee that we should be able to provide causal explanation in any particular case.

On the other hand a teleological explanation of the events described in our example might be given by the statement that antelopes *exist for the purpose* of sustaining lions. Generally speaking a teleological explanation of the sequence of two events consists in a statement that all or some of the things involved in the first exist for the purpose of all or some of the things involved in the second. (While a causal explanation presupposes at least a sequence of two distinguishable events a teleological explanation is possible in the case of a single event involving more than one thing. It would consist in stating that one or more of them exist for the sake of some other.)

From what has been said so far it is clear already that a teleological explanation is quite different from a causal one. The latter does not, strictly speaking, explain *why* (= for what purpose) events happen or things exist, but only how. Indeed from a completely mechanistic point of view the question *why* events happen or things exist would be illegitimate, because it is in principle unanswerable. The same sequence of events may be capable both of a causal and a teleological explanation. The latter is then, as it were, superimposed upon the former. The antelope's coming close to the lion and its subsequently being killed is then first explained as an instance of a causal connexion which in turn is teleologically explained by the statement that antelopes exist for the purpose of being food for lions. Frequently, however, it is the sequence of events itself and not their causal connectedness that is teleologically explained.

Cases which are likely to remain incapable of causal explanation often seem to urge us to attempt direct teleological explanation. Whether we resist this urge or succumb to it is here not relevant. 'Experience', as Kant puts it,[1] 'leads our Judgement ... to the notion of a purpose in nature only if what is to be judged is a relation between cause and effect and if we are unable to see their necessary connexion [*als gesetzlich einzusehen*] by any means except by ... making the Idea of the effect into the condition of the possibility of the cause.'

The purposiveness which we thus see in, or project into, nature, is either an *outer* purposiveness, as in our example, where one thing serves the purpose of a different thing; or else it is an *inner* purposiveness which is characteristic of one whole thing. The former 'is merely relative and ... accidental to the thing to which it is attributed'[2] and is expressed by 'hypothetical' judgements. The latter is ascribed to living organisms. An organism is, so to speak, a purpose unto itself – *a purpose in nature (Naturzweck)* without qualification, and not merely a relative one. The peculiarly intimate interdependence between the parts and the whole of an organism is expressed by 'absolute teleological judgements'.[3]

The notion of an organism is characterized as follows: *First*, a thing is an organism only if 'the existence and form of its parts ... [are] possible only through their relation to the whole'.[4] The description has a verisimilitude. The existence and form of a hand, say, may indeed quite plausibly be considered impossible in separation from the body to which it belongs. *Second* – and again Kant's description seems convincing – the parts of an organism constitute 'the unity of a whole by being mutually the cause and effect of their form'. Lastly, many organisms, and only organisms, have the power of reproducing themselves.

An organism is thus not only an organized thing but also a thing organizing itself. In a mechanism the parts are conditions of each other's function. In an organism they also exist through each other and in a sense produce each other. A blade of grass is quite different from a clock, which does not grow

1. *Ju.* 366.   2. *Ju.* 368.   3. *Ju.* 369.   4. *Ju.* 373.

or produce other clocks. An organism 'is thus not merely a machine: for that has only *moving power*; but it also has within itself a *formative power* with which it endows the various kinds of matter which lack it (thereby organizing them) . . .'[1]

So far the argument has only shown (1) that the notion of purposes in nature is in fact being employed, and that (2) our incapacity, temporary or perhaps permanent, of providing a satisfactory causal explanation of certain natural phenomena inclines us to make use of it. It is now time, as we have done so often before, to leave these evidences of our 'possession' of the notion and to consider whether or in what way our use of it is justifiable. We have to recall the well-documented warning of the *Dialectic of Pure Reason* that an established and logically quite clear use of a general notion may yet lack justification and be the source of contradictions and confusions.

Kant, we remember, distinguishes between *a posteriori* concepts which are abstracted from and exemplified in sense-experience; *a priori* concepts which characterize the structure of the *a priori* particulars of space and time; Categories (and concepts deducible from them) which though not abstracted from sense-experience are yet through their schemata applicable to it; and lastly Ideas which are *a priori* but incapable of being schematized and thus are inapplicable to what is given in experience. Now the notion of a purpose in nature is certainly neither an *a posteriori* concept nor a characteristic of the structure of space or time. Just as in a sequence of events we perceive one event and then another but do not also perceive the one as causing the other, so when the things or parts involved in a sequence exist for the purpose of each other we perceive only the things, not the purpose. In this respect the notions of causal and of teleological connexion are similar.

There is, however, a very important point in which they differ. The Category of causal connexion can be schematized; the notion of a purpose in nature cannot. To schematize a Category is, we remember, to exhibit the temporal conditions of its applicability – permanence in the case of Substance,

1. *Ju.* 374.

existence at a certain time in the case of Reality, etc. The schema of Causality consists 'in the succession of the manifold in so far as it is subject to a rule'.[1] Regular succession, in other words, is a perceptual feature in the absence of which there can be no causal connexion. Teleological connexion is not similarly linked to a temporal condition or, for that matter, to any other definite feature of pure or empirical perception. We cannot indicate any necessary perceptual condition for the application of 'purpose in nature'. The notion has no schema.

The *a priori* notion of a purpose in nature must therefore be an Idea. Indeed in saying that a particular thing is an organism we are referring to a relationship between the parts and the whole which is to us an utter mystery. It is not causal and is 'strictly speaking not analogous to any causality which we know'.[2] We can in a similar manner say that man *qua* noumenon is morally free; but the Idea of moral freedom must remain mysterious to us – even if we can prove that it is internally consistent and implied by the categorical imperative. Although Ideas are thus not applied to experience they may yet be usefully employed in our thought. This has been shown in the first *Critique* for the Ideas of Pure Reason and can also be shown for the Idea of purpose in nature.

The Categories of the Understanding are governed by synthetic *a priori* principles which are the conditions of objective empirical judgements and indeed of the experience of objects. Ideas are not in this sense constitutive (i.e. constitutive of objects). They may, however, have a regulative function which is expressed not by synthetic *a priori* judgements but by *maxims* which are subjective principles based not on the characteristics of an object but on the 'interest of reason to confer a certain possible perfection on the knowledge of the objects'.[3] The maxims which express the regulative function of the Ideas of Pure Reason are rules the observation of which enables us to progress towards an increasing unification of our empirical judgements into a system.[4]

1. *Pu. R.* 138, *B* 184.   2. *Ju.* 375.
3. *Pu. R.* 440, *B* 694.   4. See Ch. v, § 5.

The Idea of a purpose in nature also can have a regulative function in so far as it is employed in accordance with 'a remote analogy to our causality with respect to our own purposes [*mit unserer Causalität nach Zwecken*]';[1] in other words, in so far as its use is remotely analogous to the use of the notion of a human purpose. The maxim governing the regulative use of the Idea is called by Kant 'the *maxim* for judging the inner purposiveness of organized beings'.[2] This maxim, which according to him is at the same time the definition of an organism, he formulates thus: 'An organized product of nature is that in which everything is reciprocally both means and end.'[3]

From it there follow two corollaries which as methodological rules are, at least for heuristic reasons, observed by biologists, namely (a) the maxim that 'nothing in such a being exists *in vain*' and (b) the maxim that 'nothing happens *merely by accident* [*von ungefähr*, without purpose]'. Since maxims are rules of procedure it would be more precise to say that they enjoin us to proceed on the assumption that, or better still *as if*, nothing in an organism existed in vain or happened merely by accident. All this does not prejudge the possibility of explaining *some* parts or functions of an organism by merely mechanistic laws.

In judging things as organisms or purposes in nature we are transcending possible sense-experience: for such experience can be characterized only by means of *a posteriori* or schematized *a priori* concepts. If we use teleological explanation in situations where the other is unavailable we can – limited by the same provisos – go further and judge even those products of nature 'which do not require us to go beyond the mechanism of blindly efficient causes . . . as belonging to a system of purposes'.[4] That is to say, if and in so far as a direct teleological explanation of natural phenomena is possible the superimposition of a teleological on a causal explanation is also possible.

Teleological Judgement thus enables us to unite the realm of nature and the realm of purposes into one system. It enables us to bridge the gap between the conception of man as a

1. *Ju.* 375.   2. *Ju.* 376.   3. *Loc. cit.*   4. *Ju.* 380.

phenomenal and causally determined being and as a morally free agent. 'Neither of man nor indeed of any rational being in the world as a moral being can we [as we can in the case of other organisms] ... ask why (*quem ad finem*) he exists ... Only in man as the subject of morality do we find unconditioned legislation with respect to purposes – a legislation which makes him capable of being an ultimate purpose to which the whole of nature is subordinated.'[1]

Moreover, once 'such a clue for the study of nature', namely teleological explanation, 'has been adopted and found useful [*bewährt*] we must at least try to apply this maxim of Judgement in our reflection about nature as a whole ...'[2] We are then, whether philosophers or not, led to the assumption that the universe 'depends on and has its source in an intelligent being ... which exists outside the world: that teleology thus can find no completion of its inquiries except in a theology'.[3]

Many important metaphysical systems based on various notions of natural purpose, final cause, or organism do indeed require that God's existence be assumed. This is so in the metaphysics of Aristotle and Aquinas and in Whitehead's 'philosophy of organism'. As Whitehead points out,[4] it is an especially important fact in the history of metaphysics that 'Aristotle found it necessary to complete his metaphysics by the introduction of a Prime Mover – God'. It is important not only because he was a very great thinker but mainly because 'in his consideration of this metaphysical question he was entirely dispassionate; and he is the last European metaphysician of first-rate importance for whom this claim can be made'.

Within the context of Aristotle's or Aquinas's thought the view is natural that we need teleology and that teleology leads to theology. It may seem strange if such a view is expressed by the author of the critical philosophy, 'the great destroyer in the realm of thought', as Heine calls him, the thinker 'whose terrorism by far exceeded that of Maximilien Robespierre'. The impression of strangeness arises, however, only if we

1. *Ju.* 435.   2. *Ju.* 398.   3. *Ju.* 399.
4. *Science and the Modern World*, Ch. XI.

forget that the notion of purposes in nature is an Idea and that the principles governing its employment are only maxims of reflective Judgement and not empirical generalizations or synthetic *a priori* principles.

Kant himself sees to it that we do not forget this. 'What', he asks,[1] 'can in the end be proved by even the most complete teleology? Does it perhaps prove that such an intelligent being exists? No, it proves no more than this, that – our cognitive faculties being what they are – we cannot at all form the conception of such a world [i.e. a teleologically organized one] unless we regard an intentionally acting being as its supreme cause.' Kant does not reinstate the older teleological metaphysics. He tries to show that its doctrines are not true of objective reality in the scientific sense but arise from certain modes of thought which are, so he believes, unavoidably adopted by man when he reflects about the phenomena of life and his own experience. If it be objected that even the application of the Categories does, according to the critical philosophy, remove us from the things in themselves, his answer would, I think, have to be that the employment of Ideas removes us still further from them.

3. Mechanism and Teleology

In his discussion of the relation between mechanistic and teleological explanation Kant remains faithful to his method of dealing with Ideas, a method which he has handled successfully and elegantly in the other parts of the critical philosophy, especially in the Dialectic of Pure Reason. It consists in the formulation and resolution of an antinomy. Here it is the antinomy of teleological Judgement. Its thesis is the statement 'All production of material things *is possible* according to mere mechanistic laws'. Its antithesis says 'some production of such things *is not possible* in accordance with merely mechanistic laws'.[2] The two statements are straight contradictories and cannot therefore both be true.

1. *Ju.* 399.   2. *Ju.* 387, my italics.

The contradiction arises from careless formulation, or from neglecting the fundamental difference between statements of fact or possibility and *maxims* which are rules of procedure. As regards the latter even conflicting maxims can profitably be observed to a certain extent or 'up to a point' by the same person. If we remember this we must replace the statement of the thesis by the maxim ' All production of material things and their forms *must be considered* [*beurtheilt*] *as* being possible in accordance with merely mechanistic laws'; and we must replace the statement of the antithesis by the maxim, 'Some products of material nature *cannot be considered* in accordance with merely mechanistic laws (their consideration [*Beurtheilung*] requires an altogether different law of causality, namely, that of final causes).'[1]

The contradiction has now vanished. The first maxim prescribes that I should *reflect* upon all events in material nature 'according to the principle of a mere mechanism of nature and consequently push my investigation with it as far as I can . . .'[2] It does not prevent me, logically or in fact, from proceeding, when occasion arises, in accordance with the second maxim, the maxim of teleological explanation. Kant's argument here shows some similarity to a device which has forced itself on contemporary physicists who, without contradiction, *consider* the propagation of light in some contexts *as* wave motion, in others as the motion of particles.

Kant's resolution of the antinomy of reflective Judgement must be considered in the light of the first *Critique*. In that work, especially in the Analytic of Principles, he has expounded a system of theoretical *a priori* propositions which constitute the fundamental conditions of Newtonian physics and, in his view, of all science. The result of the first *Critique* is thus, among other things, a mechanistic metaphysics; and nothing in the *Critique of Judgement* indicates that Kant has in any way changed his view on this subject.[3]

1. *Loc. cit.*, my italics.   2. *Ju.* 387.
3. We must remember here that according to Kant all metaphysics which is not a mere illusion consists of propositions which are necessary conditions of objective experience.

To a mechanistic metaphysics there corresponds a mechanistic method of inquiry. If the phenomenal world 'stands under' the synthetic *a priori* principles of the Understanding which are constitutive of the empirical world; if, in other words, the empirical world *is* a mechanistic system, then it is reasonable to act *as if* it were such a system and to adopt the *maxim* of mechanistic inquiry.

The third *Critique* does *not* develop a teleological metaphysics. On the contrary, it shows that teleological principles are *not* constitutive of the empirical world, but can only be regulative for our reflection upon the empirical world. While the first *Critique* justifies the mechanistic method on the basis of a mechanistic metaphysic, the *third* Critique justifies the teleological method in spite of the impossibility of a teleological metaphysic. This impossibility is insisted upon time and again. Kant admits only a metaphysic of nature and a metaphysic of morals. There is no metaphysic of purpose, but only a *Critique of Teleological Judgement*.[1] He shows that there is no conflict between the maxims of mechanistic and teleological method. There can be no conflict between mechanistic and teleological metaphysics because, according to the critical philosophy, there can be no teleological metaphysics.

The value of the teleological method lies not only in its use outside scientific inquiry – for the unification of nature, morals, and indeed religious faith into one system. It has also an important heuristic use within the field of mechanistic and, perhaps more generally, non-teleological science. The question for what purpose a thing exists and the teleological answer to it may indeed suggest new mechanistic explanations. 'For where purposes are considered as the conditions of the possibility of certain things, means have to be assumed . . .' and it is, as Kant points out, quite possible that the relation between means and end may 'considered *by itself* require nothing which involves a purpose'. It may indeed be both 'mechanistic and yet a subordinate cause of intended effects'.[2]

The question how far purely mechanistic explanation can go

1. See, e.g., Prefaces to *Gr.* and *Ju.*   2. *Ju.* 414.

cannot be decided *a priori*, and Kant certainly does not think that it can. In our own day when the invention of electronic 'brains' and of self-regulating and self-adapting machines is by serious thinkers[1] expected to bring about another industrial revolution, we are inclined to believe that mechanistic explanation can be pushed very much further than Kant considered possible. Biologists today would not, I am told, be too surprised if the growth of a blade of grass were explained on purely mechanistic principles – not perhaps by a biological Newton, but by a team of competent research workers.

We must not forget that Kant lived before Darwin. Yet, in spite of the comparatively limited success of mechanistic explanation in his own days, he does not reject the main ideas of the theory later developed by Darwin. The passage concerned with these ideas is very often quoted. Nevertheless I venture to put it down again (in Meredith's translation): 'When we consider the agreement of so many genera of animals in a certain common schema, which apparently underlies not only the structure of their bones, but also the disposition of their remaining parts, and when we find here the wonderful simplicity of the original plan, which has been able to produce such an immense variety of species by the shortening of one member and the lengthening of another, by the involution of this part and the evolution of that, there gleams upon the mind a ray of hope, however faint, that the principle of the mechanism in nature, apart from which there can be no natural science at all, may yet enable us to arrive at some explanation in the case of organic life.'[2]

I cannot forbear to quote in addition part of a footnote which makes Kant's biological views still clearer. 'An hypothesis of this kind may be called a daring adventure on the part of reason; and there are probably few among the most acute scientists to whose minds it has not sometimes occurred. For it cannot be said to be absurd, like the *generatio aequivoca*, which means the generation of an organized being from crude

1. See, e.g., N. Wiener, *Cybernetics*, New York, 1948, p. 37.
2. *Ju.* 418.

inorganic matter . . .' It would not be absurd to suppose that 'certain water animals transformed themselves by degrees into marsh-animals, and from these after some generations into land animals. In the judgement of plain reason there is nothing *a priori* self-contradictory in this. But experience offers no example of it . . .'[1]

The following seems a fair summary of Kant's theory of teleological explanation: the third *Critique* implies, no less than the first, that all explanation must be mechanistic, but it supplements its theses. Even within the field of scientific inquiry mechanistic explanation has its limits, although one cannot prophesy at what point it will break down. Kant, quite naturally, believes that this will happen much earlier than contemporary biologists are inclined to assume. His conjectures, however, that certain phenomena, e.g. the growth of organisms or the affinity between different species, are not susceptible to mechanistic explanation, do not form part of the critical philosophy. They are *obiter dicta* expressing his strong interest in the science of his day and his expectation of its progress. Teleological principles, unlike mechanistic, are not constitutive of objects, but merely regulative. Within scientific inquiry they suggest mechanistic questions and answers. Their main function, however, is the unification into one system of our thinking about matters of fact and of moral and religious experience. If Kant hankered after the old teleological metaphysics, his published works show no evidence of it. I do not think that he did.

Kant's philosophy of the biological sciences is, as far as I can judge, by no means outmoded. This is best shown by quoting from the writings of contemporary biologists whose general outlook differs from his. Thus Dr Needham[2] subscribes to a view which he calls Neo-mechanism. According to him 'the neomechanistic position . . . at one and the same time asserting the universal dominion of the mechanical sort of explanation over all nature, living and non-living, and ad-

1. *Ju.* 420.
2. *The Sceptical Biologist*, London, 1929, pp. 204 ff.

mitting the inadequate nature of this sort of explanation as a
full account of the world, resembles the old mechanisticism in
maintaining the heuristic need for the machine, and differs
from it in seeing nothing solely ultimate about the machine.
It thus recognizes itself to be the way the scientific mind goes
to work, and not the manner of thinking in philosophy,
theology, or art . . . It knows teleology to be an unquantitative
category, and banishes it from the laboratory to the domain of
the philosophers, who are quite capable of dealing with it . . .
It may be noted that such a standpoint as Neo-mechanism will
not necessarily object to special "biological" laws or explanations, provided that they are clearly understood to possess an
"interim" character and to be only awaiting expression in
physico-chemical terms.' Dr Needham finds that the neomechanistic position stands in close relationship with the
Hegelian views put forward by R. G. Collingwood in his
book *Speculum Mentis*; they are really found before either
Collingwood or Hegel in the *Critique of Judgement*. There is
only one major point of difference: the sceptical biologist is
much less sceptical than Kant was about the 'interim' character of all special biological laws.

Another contemporary biologist, von Bertalanffy,[1] shows
less sympathy for any kind of teleology; but his views about
the limits of physico-chemical explanation are similar to those
expressed in the third *Critique*. 'Just because we are champion-
ing exact, theoretical and quantitative biology we have', he
says, 'to point out that what is expressed in the "exact"
sciences as "laws" represents only a small section of reality . . .
As mathematical biologists, we put the greatest emphasis on
the obedience of organic forms to exact laws . . . But for precisely this reason we know only too well that it is only a small
part of phenomena that can be understood in an "exact" way.
Two skulls are distinguished not only by coarse differences of
proportion which we can measure and calculate, but also by a
wealth of characteristics that can only be described in verbal
language, or even are noticed only by the morphologist's

1. *Problems of Life*, London, 1952, pp. 152 ff.

trained eye, but which he is hardly able to put into words.'
The question of 'biological mechanism' relates only to 'those
general traits of order which we are able to state in the form
of "laws"'.

Contemporary philosophers are inclined to formulate the
problem of the relation between mechanistic and teleological
explanation as the question whether teleological statements
can be 'reduced to' non-teleological ones. The answer, of
course, depends largely on what is meant by such a 'reduction'. If the conditions for a successful reduction are sufficiently lax then almost any type of statement will be reducible
to any other. If they are very strict then no type of statement
will be reducible to any other. Teleological statements about
human purposes and intentions do not, as we have seen, present any great difficulty since the intention or the making of a
plan clearly precedes the activities which are explained as being
caused by it.

R. B. Braithwaite and others have shown that in many contexts goal-directed behaviour on the part of organisms can be
explained without resort to teleology. Braithwaite argues that
such behaviour can be explained in terms of plasticity which
'is a property of the organism with respect to a certain goal,
namely that the organism can attain the same goal under different circumstances by alternative forms of activity making use
frequently of different causal chains'. The 'reduction' of teleological statements about final causes to plasticity-statements
about alternative causal chains leading to the same effect is
performed with admirable clarity and in great detail.[1] Kant's
position is quite compatible with this and similar reductions –
as long as it is understood that they are to be employed *within*
the natural sciences.

In so far, however, as a philosopher must consider not only
science, but other types of experience such as art and morals;
and in so far as he must consider them together, teleological
explanation is not 'reducible' to mechanical. The inquiry into
how we can for certain purposes and within a limited field of

1. See *Scientific Explanation*, Cambridge, 1953, Ch. x.

experience do without teleology must then give way to an inquiry how in our thinking we employ the notion of (non-human) purpose, and what kind of truth or objectivity, if any, we can achieve by doing so. The *Critique of Teleological Judgement* is such an inquiry.

4. Opinion, Knowledge, and Faith

The arduous task of the *Critique* of reason had been undertaken in the hope of finding some answer to the three great metaphysical problems of moral freedom, the immortality of the soul, and the existence of God. In the course of the inquiry many new and important problems had to be formulated and their solution attempted, and there is hardly a major philosophical issue which has been left without examination. The three great problems of metaphysics themselves appear in an entirely new light whatever we may think of the solution to them which Kant suggests in the Dialectic of Pure Reason and the second *Critique*. Towards the end of the *Critique of Judgement* Kant briefly considers them again by means of a distinction between three types of knowledge, in a wide sense of the term.

Kant distinguishes between matters of opinion, matters of fact, and matters of faith. *Matters of opinion* are 'objects of an empirical knowledge which is at least in principle possible . . . [*einer wenigstens an sich möglichen Erfahrungserkenntnis*], but is [in fact] impossible *for us* because the degree to which we are capable of empirical cognition is not sufficiently high'.[1] In order to illustrate this definition Kant gives two examples. His first example of a matter of opinion is the assumption that other planets are inhabited by rational beings. The reason why we cannot verify or falsify it lies in purely technical limitations which may or may not one day be overcome. The difference between verifying whether the house next door, the north pole, or Mars is inhabited is one of degree.

1. *Ju.* 468.

Kant's second example is the assumption made by some physicists of his day (and, we may add, of the early twentieth century) that there is an ether, i.e. an elastic liquid which penetrates all substances. Although the existence of such a liquid cannot, and is not meant to be, verified or falsified by any experiment or observation, such a test would according to Kant be possible 'if our external senses were sharpened to the highest degree',[1] which, however, can never happen. The now obsolete concept of an ether belongs to the same class as the concepts 'gene', 'atomic nucleus', and others which although unexemplifiable in sense-experience, are yet essential to certain empirical theories.

These 'semi-empirical' concepts, as we might call them, cut across the Kantian classification of all general notions into *a posteriori* and *a priori* concepts and Ideas of reason. Kant's attempt to assimilate them to *a posteriori* concepts and to assimilate all statements about their *imperceivable* instances to matters of opinion does not seem convincing. After the fashion of some medieval logicians, Brentano and Russell regarded semi-empirical concepts, together with many other constituents of propositions, as syncategorematic terms (incomplete symbols). Such terms *do not have instances*, as have empirical concepts, but they may nevertheless contribute to the meaning of empirical propositions containing them. I cannot, for example, meaningfully say, 'This is an atomic nucleus', although the proposition 'The explosion of an atomic bomb is the result of changes involving atomic nuclei' has empirical meaning and although certain statements about the structure of atoms are matters of scientific opinion.

This is not the place to expound or to develop a theory of semi-empirical terms or, more generally, of incomplete symbols. But the absence of any such theory in the critical philosophy is certainly worth noting. There is no evidence that Kant ever even considered it, and it is idle to speculate how far it would have affected his system, in particular the Transcendental Analytic of Concepts. I do not, however, believe that

1. *Loc. cit.*

it would have made the distinction which Kant draws between different types of concept superfluous.

Matters of fact are instances of concepts 'the objective reality of which can be demonstrated (be it through pure reason or experience) and in the former case either from theoretical or practical data of reason; in all cases, however, by means of a perception which corresponds to the concept'.[1] To prove the reality of a concept or, what comes to the same, that an instance of it exists as a matter of fact, is thus (1) to make clear the logical content of the concept by means of empirical or *a priori* principles, (2) to indicate an instance of it in one's own or other people's experience. This wide sense of the term 'matter of fact' which, as Kant himself admits, goes beyond its ordinary meaning, covers historical, mathematical, and scientific statements.

It also makes – what Kant considers 'very remarkable' – the statement that man is free a statement of fact. This is so because we can demonstrate the reality of the Idea of freedom (1) by means of practical *a priori* principles, and (2) by indicating actions, i.e. perceivable events happening in space and time, which correspond to it. But moral freedom is not a scientific fact, a matter of fact in the sense of theoretical reason. It is no more, but also no less, than a moral or practical fact in the sense explained by the second *Critique*.

Even Kant's wide definitions of 'matters of fact' and of the correlative 'reality of a concept' cover the Idea only of freedom, not any other Ideas. The objects which correspond to the others and which are not given in experience are *matters of faith* which 'must be thought as related to the employment of pure practical reason in the service of duty' but which 'transcend the theoretical use of reason'.[2] These Ideas are the highest good – the just proportion between virtue and happiness – and what Kant believes to be the only possible conditions of its achievement, namely the immortality of the soul and the existence of God. Faith is 'a confidence in the achievement of a purpose, the promotion of which is a duty; but we

1. *Ju.* 469. 2. *Loc. cit.*

can have no *insight* into the manner in which this purpose could be realized . . .'[1] Faith thus is neither a matter of knowledge, nor of opinion, but is 'wholly a matter of morality'[2] – one of the things which Kant never tires of urging whenever occasion offers.

Aesthetic and teleological notions and judgements do not fall within the region of factual knowledge, of opinion, or of faith. They belong to man's creative powers, his capacity to become aware of beauty and to produce it, and his capacity to impose order and system upon his perception and thought. They are used in his attempts to reach the unknown and even the unknowable.

We have come to the end of this introduction to Kant's philosophy. I have tried to present its main theses and their connexion with each other and to point out their relevance to contemporary problems. One main aim of the undertaking has been to show that no one who takes these problems or indeed philosophy seriously can without much loss to himself ignore Kant's teaching. I should, therefore, like to conclude by expressing the hope that my exposition, brief and inadequate as in the nature of the case it has had to be, has not greatly misrepresented the thought of a very great thinker.

1. *Ju.* 474.　　　　2. *Loc. cit.*

Some Notes on Kant's Life and Personality

THE main sources of information on Kant's life and personality are his correspondence[1] and three biographical sketches by his friends L. E. Borowski, R. B. Jachmann, and E. A. C. Wasianski, published in 1804, the year of Kant's death. In reading these biographies one can hardly avoid an impression that the admiration and reverence which the writers felt for their great friend blunted their powers of characterization. They were writing of the aged Kant, the man who had done his work, rather than of the adventurous thinker advancing into it. A lively and credible account of Kant at the height of his powers is contained in a recent monograph by K. Stavenhagen.[2]

Kant was born in 1724, in Königsberg, where his father was a saddler. Before attending the University he spent eight years at the *Collegium Fridericianum* where he was given a grammar school training. At Königsberg University he studied mainly philosophy and mathematics, but also theology and physics. After finishing his University studies he spent some years as a private tutor, as did many philosophers before and after him. His own opinion of his aptitude for this profession was low.

At the age of thirty-one came an appointment as *Magister legens (Privatdozent)*. In this position Kant was financially dependent on fees paid by his students and his income was at times so small that he was forced to supplement it by selling parts of his library. In 1770 he was appointed to a professorship of logic and metaphysics, at the University, and although he was several times offered posts elsewhere, he was never

1. See *Akademie* edition, *Briefe*.
2. *Kant und Königsberg*, Göttingen, 1948.

induced to leave his native city. Kant was a prolific writer and made important contributions to subjects outside philosophy. In a cosmological essay (1755) he expressed ideas similar to those expressed later by Laplace. They are known as the Kant-Laplace theory of the origin of the universe and consist in the application of Newton's principles to the question of cosmogony. The long list of his writings is contained in most histories of philosophy.

Between 1775 and 1781 Kant did not publish anything of importance. He was then working on what was to become the *Critique of Pure Reason*, the first edition of which appeared in 1781. The reception of the book was a great disappointment to him. The contemporary philosophers whose judgement he valued most took little notice. Mendelssohn declared that he could not follow the argument and 'his nervous debility' forbade him 'all exertion'.[1] Within a few years, however, the *Critique of Pure Reason* was recognized as the important work it was; and like all of Kant's later works, has never ceased to exert a great influence on philosophers of all schools.

The city of Königsberg owed its importance to its trade with Poland, Lithuania, England, Denmark, and Sweden. Its inhabitants, though mainly German, included people of different nationalities, among them business men from the British Isles. Two of these, Green and Motherby, were among Kant's most intimate friends. Kant was fond of his home town, in which, as he puts it, knowledge of men and the world 'can be acquired even without travel'.[2]

Kant gave lectures not only on logic, metaphysics and paedagogics, the last of which according to University regulation had to be taken by each of the professors in turn, but also on 'physics, natural law, ethics, rational theology, anthropology, and physical geography'. Some of the lectures had to be based on approved text-books which, however, as Jachmann tells us, 'he used only by following their general division

1. Letter of 10.4.1783.
2. See preface to the *Anthropology*, quoted by Stavenhagen *loc. cit.*

and taking at times the opportunity of demonstrating that their theses were impermissible'. Kant's lectures, unlike his books, were full of wit, humour, and interesting digressions. He took a warm interest in the well-being of his students and they in turn felt an affection for him which long outlasted their student days. He was a strict examiner. His guiding principle as a teacher of philosophy was to teach his students not so much philosophical doctrines as how to philosophize.

Kant was a loyal friend and an entertaining companion. He went every day to his friend Green's home to spend a few hours with him and other friends as long as Green was alive. He enjoyed good food and intelligent conversation, though the conversation, according to report, almost never touched upon philosophy. Like most other people, and in particular most philosophers, he did not relish being persistently contradicted. He liked the company of good-looking, well-educated ladies, and was liked by them. In his old age he never regretted having remained a bachelor.

I have made some remarks, above, on Kant's aesthetic taste.[1] He had a great love for the writers of classical antiquity. Among moderns he thought highly of Haller, Pope, and Milton. He was very fond of Hume as a philosopher and writer. He was also a great admirer of Rousseau and knew all his works very well. They could at times profoundly excite him. When the *Emile* first came into his hands he even for some time omitted to take his regular daily walks! I have tried[2] to say something of Rousseau's influence on the Kantian ethics. In educational matters his influence is revealed among other things in Kant's very active support of the '*Philanthropin*' in Dessau, a school which broke with many educational traditions. His reading was very wide, but he avoided 'theological disquisitions of any kind, especially those relating to exegesis and dogmatics' (this does not refer to *rational* theology, which was part of metaphysics; see Jachmann). Certain kinds of aesthetic taste seem to have remained wholly uncultivated by him. He regarded music as 'innocent pleasure of the senses'.

1. See Ch. VIII.   2. Ch. VI.

He seems never to have noticed paintings and engravings, even those which to Jachmann appeared to be 'of excellent quality'. An engraving of Rousseau in his living-room was the only picture in his house.

His interest in the political events of his day was very great. In the American War of Independence his sympathies were with the Americans. When Königsberg was occupied in the most humane manner by the Russians in the Seven Years' War,[1] he like most other citizens of the town went quietly about his own business, lecturing to educated Russian officers as he had done before to Prussian. He even applied to the Tsarina for a professorship as he had done before to the king of Prussia. The Seven Years' War was certainly not 'ideological'.

'Since the time of the French Revolution,' Jachmann tells us, 'perhaps nothing has caused so great a sensation or made for their author so many friends and enemies as Kant's political principles and opinions.' He believed that the best form of government was a republic or constitutional monarchy with a strict separation of the legislative from the executive power. He believed in the rights of man, in civil liberty and equality. It was, therefore, natural that he should show a passionate interest in a revolution with the aims of which he sympathized so much. His was, as his biographer puts it, 'the pure interest of a citizen of the world and an independent philosopher, who looked at the experiment which was intended to realize ... the Idea of a perfect constitution, with the same delight as would a natural scientist who observed an experiment which is to confirm an important hypothesis'.

Kant, however, was a loyal subject of his state in spite of the fact that he disagreed with many of the principles by which it was ruled and in spite of the fact that he had at one time to suffer under its narrow-minded censorship. When the Abbé Sieyès offered, through a clergyman from the neighbouring town of Memel, to enter into correspondence with him he refused this offer as incompatible with his duties as a citizen.

1. See Stavenhagen *loc. cit.*

Kant was never really ill, though he was never a person of robust health. The sharp deterioration of his intellectual powers in the last six years of his life was a great sorrow to him. Three years before his death in 1804 he resigned his place in the senate of his university. He died on the twenty-eighth of February, of that year, in Königsberg, where with hardly an interruption he had spent his whole life. His bodily remains have been interred since 1880 under a simple Gothic chapel near the cathedral.

Some Notes on the Editions and Translations of Kant's Works

The standard German edition of Kant's published works, correspondence, and literary remains has been provided by the *Preussische Akademie der Wissenschaften* (22 volumes, Berlin, 1902, etc., second edition 1910, etc.). Most English translations appearing since then refer to this edition of his works.

Other editions: E. Cassirer and others (10 vols., Berlin, 1912–22; G. Hartenstein (8 vols., Leipzig, 1867–8); G. Hartenstein (10 vols., Leipzig, 1938–9); Rosenkranz and Schubert (12 vols., Leipzig, 1838–42); Vorländer and others (10 vols., Philos. Bibl., Felix Meiner, 1914, etc.). There are many separate editions of the three *Critiques* and of other works.

Some English translations of the main works which are at present available: (a) *Critique of Pure Reason*: N. Kemp Smith (London, 1929); (b) *Prolegomena*: L. W. Beck (Indianapolis, 1950); J. W. Ellington (Indianapolis, 1977); P. G. Lucas (Manchester, 1953); (c) *Critique of Practical Reason*: L. W. Beck (Indianapolis, 1956); (d) *Foundations of (Grounding for) the Metaphysics of Morals*: L. W. Beck (Indianapolis, 1959); J. W. Ellington (Indianapolis, 1981); (e) *Critique of Judgment*: J. H. Bernard (New York, 1951); J. C. Meredith (Oxford, 1952). There are other translations of these and other works.

SOME ENGLISH COMMENTARIES

Books and commentaries on Kant's philosophy are very numerous in most languages, especially in German. I shall here mention only some important commentaries that have appeared in the present century in English. The reader of any of these can, if he feels so inclined, follow the threads of references and thus find his bearings in the extensive field of Kantian scholarship and literature.

(a) *Critique of Pure Reason*: L. W. Beck, *Studies in the Philosophy of Kant* (Indianapolis, 1965); J. Bennett, *Kant's Analytic* (Cambridge, 1966), *Kant's Dialectic* (Cambridge, 1974); G. G. Brittan, *Kant's Theory of Science* (Princeton, 1978); C. D. Broad, *Kant: An Introduction* (Cambridge, 1978); A. C. Ewing, *A Short Commentary on Kant's Critique of Pure Reason* (2nd ed., London, 1950); N. Kemp Smith, *A Commentary to Kant's Critique of Pure Reason* (London, 1918); J. H. Paton, *Kant's Metaphysic of Experience—A Commentary on the First Half of the Kritik der reinen Vernunft*, 2 vols. (London, 1936); P. F. Strawson, *The Bounds of Sense: An Essay on Kant's Critique of Pure Reason* (London, 1966); W. H. Walsh, *Kant's Criticism of Metaphysics* (New York, 1975); T. E. Wilkerson, *Kant's Critique of Pure Reason: A Commentary for Students* (Oxford, 1976).

(b) *Moral Philosophy*: L. W. Beck, *Commentary on Kant's Critique of Practical Reason* (Chicago, 1960); M. Despland, *Kant on History and Religion* (Montreal and London, 1973); J. H. Paton, *The Categorical Imperative—A Study in Kant's Moral Philosophy* (London, 1947); R. P. Wolff, *The Autonomy of Reason: A Commentary on Kant's Groundwork of the Metaphysic of Morals* (New York, 1973).

(c) *Critique of Judgment*: H. W. Cassirer, *A Commentary on Kant's Critique of Judgment* (London, 1938); D. W. Crawford, *Kant's Aesthetic Theory* (Madison, Wis., 1974); P. Guyer, *Kant and the Claims of Taste* (Cambridge, Mass., 1979); P. MacFarland, *Kant's Concept of Teleology* (Edinburgh and New York, 1971).